Timothy Gorringe is  at
the University of Exete   in
Leeds and Oxford, an   du
Theological Seminary and at the univ   nd
St Andrews. He is also a smallholder with a longstanding inter-
est in farming. Timothy Gorringe is the author of *Crime* in the
Changing Society and the Churches series, published by SPCK
(2004).

HARVEST

HARVEST

Food, Farming and the Churches

Timothy Gorringe

First published in Great Britain in 2006

Society for Promoting Christian Knowledge
36 Causton Street
London SW1P 4ST

British Library Cataloguing-in-Publication Data
A catalogue record for this book is available from the British Library

ISBN-13: 978–0–281–05817–4
ISBN-10: 0–281–05817–2

1 3 5 7 9 10 8 6 4 2

Typeset by Graphicraft Ltd, Hong Kong
Printed in Great Britain by Bookmarque Ltd, Croydon, Surrey

For Carol
1946–2004
But you like none, none you, for constant heart

Contents

———◆◆◆———

Preface

———•◦•———

A couple of years ago I was visiting a radical, politically engaged, priest in the north of England. It was September, and I asked him what he was doing for harvest. 'Oh, we don't bother with that' was his reply. The reason was given in another encounter. Asked to preach at a harvest festival I had talked about world trade. A couple accosted the vicar at the door: 'We came especially for harvest festival, but that sermon ruined it! What's it got to do with harvest?'

Harvest festival certainly used to be one of the best attended services of the year. The altar piled high with marrows, baskets of fruit, pumpkins and tins of goodness knows what to be given to the old folks' home down the road; favourite hymns: 'We plough the fields and scatter'; 'Come ye thankful people, come'. It was a feel-good service, but it was not all sentimentality. It corresponded to a sense that, after all, food and the labour which produced it were something to be thankful for. Now health and safety legislation has done for the symbolic aspect, as you are not allowed to give the produce to the old folks' home, and nobody knows what to do with marrows anymore. There is a sense, which my northern friend obviously shared, that harvest is part of that sentimental yearning for a pre-industrial past which gives us *Past Times* and the whole heritage industry – and there is some truth in that. But that sentimental gloss must not be allowed to blind us to the profound significance of harvest in a world of colossal poverty, unjust trade and climate change. In fact, harvest is one of the most momentous occasions of the year bringing together crucial political issues and reflecting on them in the light of the entire Christian faith. There is no single doctrine of the creed which is not relevant to its celebration.

Worship, of course, is like the clergy, non-utilitarian. It cannot be defended on the grounds that it recharges our batteries for the hard week ahead, nor that the sermon raises our consciousness on global issues. Worship is a response of love and praise to God our creator and redeemer. Nevertheless, because it is also a call to repentance, to taking stock, and a call to change our ways, it does raise our consciousness. The Australian philosopher Raymond Gaita tells the story of how, working in a mental hospital with good, conscientious, liberal doctors and nurses, he and they were nevertheless put to shame by a nun who gave a level of attention and care to the patients which the rest of them, be they never so well-intentioned, could not match. As an agnostic he reflected that this perhaps stemmed from the tradition of prayerfulness which formed her life.

Not many believers are like that nun, perhaps, but to be Christian *is* to have one's responses to the world shaped by worship, 'purpose free rejoicing in God' though it is. Already in the second century Irenaeus of Lyons implied that thankfulness for the gifts of creation was implicit in every eucharist, so that every eucharist, in a sense, is a harvest festival. That is true, but the Church's year, which mirrors the seasons so closely, and which has distant echoes of harvest celebrations from Mediterranean countries in both Easter and Pentecost, remains a hugely valuable marker of time, one of the key things which rescues us from the chaos of 'one damn thing after another'. In *Common Worship*, harvest is referred to as a 'local celebration' which may be kept provided it does not supersede any principal feast. In view of the immense significance of the issues involved, both theological and political, I suggest that this is to give it too small a place, and the common sense of many congregations effectively recognizes that. The purpose of what follows is to provide resources for Christian communities for thinking about the issues, and for celebrating harvest adequately, in the age of the total market.

This book is intended as a study resource for congregations and therefore, rather than litter the text with footnotes, I have indicated my debts in the Bibliography at the end.

Timothy Gorringe

1

The common treasury

---◆•◆---

Enclosing the Commons

In 1649, at the end of the English civil war, Gerrard Winstanley led a group who became known as the Diggers to dig and sow on common land at St George's Hill in Surrey. Explaining his actions he wrote:

> In the beginning of Time, the great Creator Reason, made the Earth to be a Common Treasury to preserve Beasts, Birds, Fishes, and Man, the lord that was to govern this Creation; for Man had Domination given to him, over the Beasts, Birds, and Fishes; but not one word was spoken in the beginning, That one branch of mankind should rule over another.

Winstanley opposed the private ownership of land, which he referred to as a form of 'enclosure':

> The Earth (which was made to be a Common Treasury of relief for all, both Beasts and Men) was hedged in to In-Closures by the teachers and rulers, and the others were made Servants and Slaves: And that Earth that is within this Creation made a Common Store-house for all, is bought and sold, and kept in the hands of a few, whereby the great Creator is mightily dishonoured, as if he were a respector of persons, delighting in the comfortable Livelihood of some, and rejoycing in the miserable povertie and straits of others. From the beginning it was not so.

The enclosure of which Winstanley speaks was not the appropriation of moor and forest land for agriculture, which had been going on for thousands of years, but the enclosure of the commons which had started the previous century, displacing whole communities for more profitable sheep (a tremendous irony today when sheep fleeces are worth less than what it costs to shear them!). Winstanley considered that enclosure represented a form of idolatry, a preference for the objects of creation rather than a delight in the Spirit of reason and righteousness. He was no scholar but in his pamphlets he echoes the arguments of patristic writers from Clement of Alexandria to John Chrysostom. All of them (and Winstanley in their wake) echo Stoic arguments about the commonality of all creation, in which human beings share. The Greek words for that which is common, and sharing things in common, *koinos* (common), *koinoneo* (to have a share of), *kononia* (fellowship, communion, sharing), were important in Stoic philosophy and found their way into the New Testament. In the Acts of the Apostles we learn how the early Christian community devoted itself to *koinonia* and because of that had all things in common (*koinos*). Paul speaks of this community as a *koinonia*, a fellowship, and demands therefore that a better off part must share its goods with a poorer part in an act of *koinonia* (sharing, 2 Corinthians 8.4, 9.13). The Stoics used *koinonia* to speak of the whole inherited earth, and the early Fathers followed them in this. Thus Clement writes in his book, *The Teacher*:

> It is God himself who has brought our race to a *koinonia*, by sharing Himself, first of all, and then by sending His Word to all alike, and by making all things for all. Therefore everything is common, and the rich should not grasp a greater share. The expression, then, 'I own something and I have more than enough; why should I not enjoy it?' is not worthy of a human nor does it indicate any community feeling (*koinonikon*).

In his great treatise on Naboth's vineyard, Ambrose declares that 'The earth was made in common for all' and derives this truth from the fact that we are born and die with nothing. In his commentary on 1 Corinthians John Chrysostom likewise notes that 'all this about "mine" and "thine" is mere verbiage, and does not stand for reality. For if you say the house is yours, it is a word without reality: since the very air, earth, matter, are the Creator's; and so are you too yourself who have framed it; and all other things also.'

Winstanley stood in this Stoic–Christian tradition. Like the Fathers he believed that the argument for common ownership was self-evident, a 'law of nature' which any disinterested use of reason would discover. The light of reason showed that human beings were equal, 'sons of one Father, members of one family', to be 'fed by the Earth his Mother that brought him forth'. The Stoic idea of the Logos in every human being (and indeed in every part of creation) was given a particularly Protestant twist with the idea that everyone was their own teacher by the light of reason within them. The equality thus established was of outcome and not just of opportunity and for this, like Ambrose, Winstanley appealed to scripture: The common treasury needed to be allocated 'as every portion of the land of Canaan was the Common livelihood of such and such a Tribe, and of every member in that Tribe, without exception, neither hedging in nor hedging out'.

Private property

The belief that the earth was a common treasury sat uneasily alongside ideas of private property, enshrined in Roman law, which became the common currency of Europe through the rediscovery and dissemination of this law from the tenth century onwards. By the time Winstanley wrote, his ideas were already old-fashioned, and property law was tenaciously embedded all over Europe. Where, for his tradition, it was self-evident that basic resources belonged to all, for the tradition of private property it was equally evident that people had a right to it, though quite on what grounds was unclear. These two traditions jostle uneasily together in John Locke's writings. On the one hand he agrees with the ancient tradition that 'God . . . hath given the World to Men in common . . . all the Fruits it naturally produces, and Beasts it feeds, belong to Mankind in common'. However, the benefits of creation have to be appropriated and this is done through labour. What we produce through our labour we own, and this is not held in common: 'Thus the Grass my horse has bit; the Turfs my servant has cut; and the Ore I have digged in any place where I have a right to them in common with others, become my Property, without the assignation or consent of anybody. The labour that was mine, removing them out of that common state they were in, hath fix'd my Property in them'. The key point comes, however, in the introduction of money which allows people to own more property than their labour can actually work. Money is a device which allows property to accrue to the industrious and the rational. In Locke's view it is plain

> that Men have agreed to disproportionate and unequal Possession of the Earth, they having by a tacit and voluntary consent found out a way, how a man may fairly possess more land than he himself can use the product of, by receiving in exchange for the overplus, Gold and Silver, which may be hoarded up without injury to anyone, these metals not spoiling or decaying in the hands of the Possessor.

This argument now overturns the common treasury. In the state of nature all things were common, but not all people were rational and industrious. Some (like the North American

Indians, according to Locke) were quarrelsome and conten-
tious, and did not make a proper use of their land. The earth
belongs then, not to all, but to those whose wit and industry
allows them to exploit it. This idea was to have a long history,
being the father of the neo-liberal argument that capitalism
rests on people (entrepreneurs) using their wit and intelligence
(caput). That his arguments led not only to class division but to
slavery did not worry Locke. He himself profited from the slave
trade. Beginning with the axiom of human equality, therefore,
Locke has by simple steps ended up with private property,
ownership, class and even slavery. That it was Locke who
argued thus was hugely important for he was the epitome of the
mild-mannered liberal gentleman, and a Christian apologist
to boot. From the dangerous Hobbes these arguments might
have engendered suspicion, but from Locke they seemed only
evidence of sweet reasonableness.

Something like this argument was the moral basis for the
next huge burst of the enclosure movement in Britain in the
eighteenth century. John Dyer, in his poem 'The Fleece' wrote:

> Inclose, inclose, ye swains!
> Why will you joy in common field . . . ?
> . . . In fields
> Promiscuous held all culture languishes.

And enclose they did: six million acres, about a quarter of
all cultivated land, with the result that hundreds of thousands
of labourers were dispossessed and made their way to the
cities. At the end of his life the great agricultural reformer
Arthur Young could write, in words which might be echoed
by many in the developing world today: 'I had rather that all
the commons of England were sunk in the sea, than that the
poor should in future be treated on enclosing as they have been
hitherto'.

Nationalization and privatization

The movement for enclosure did not run unopposed. Rousseau was a passionate spokesman for a world held in common, and co-operation and common ownership were a prominent theme of the nineteenth-century union movement, which began among agricultural labourers, who knew the implications of enclosure better than others. A key plank of the original programme of the Labour Party was the nationalization of land. Not even the Attlee government had the stomach for that but what we know as 'nationalization' can be understood as a countermovement to enclosure. The major means of production apart from land – water, mines, forests, energy, transport, communications, as well as health and education – were all put into common ownership. A trend of enclosure which, according to a persistent legend, went back to the Norman conquest, was reversed, and the understanding of the commons extended.

The rationale of nationalization is that some things should not be considered commodities to be bought and sold on the marketplace but rather part of a shared inheritance or rights and therefore belong to everyone. They are not there to be bought or sold for private gain. And while the government dare not touch it, a great deal of land in Britain came into a form of common ownership through the National Trust, the aims of which very much represent the idea of a 'common treasury for all'. Elsewhere, the creation of national parks embodied the same thinking, though often at the expense of indigenous populations.

This countermovement to enclosure, however, did not last long before it was subject to a furious assault at the hands of neo-liberal economists and their political followers. For the past 30 years the aim of corporations has been once more to enclose the commons through privatization, and governments everywhere have fallen over themselves to help them do it. The root of the verb 'to privatize', we should note, is the Latin *privare*, to bereave, deprive or rob. The past participle *privatus* means 'belonging to one individual' as opposed to the commons. For Ambrose the very word 'private' 'is not according to nature':

> For nature has brought forth all things for all in common. Thus God has created everything in such a way that all things be possessed in common. Nature, therefore, is the mother of common right, usurpation of private right.

Ambrose, here, is not far off Proudhon's remark that all property is theft. The rationale of privatization is the same as that of the older agricultural enclosures, namely efficiency. In the case of those older enclosures the achievements of eighteenth-century agriculture were tremendous, though they rested more on improved husbandry than on enclosure, and where enclosures were for sheep, as in the case of the Highland clearances, the motive was more blatantly profit than improvement. In the case of the present wave of enclosure the argument is much less clear. If we take the example of the British railways, the taxpayer now pays far more in subsidies to the private companies which run them than he or she did when they were publicly owned, with the difference that taxes now go to line the pockets of private company bosses and their shareholders, a classic example of redistribution from poor to rich. As everyone who uses the railways knows, gains in efficiency are far from obvious.

The question of enclosure versus the common treasury, in the broadest sense, will be a recurring one in this book, particularly with respect to water (Chapter 4) and to knowledge (Chapter 7). The idea of the common treasury, I want to argue, is fundamental to an understanding of harvest, of a Christian approach to food and farming. Unless we get this right nothing else will come right. In relation to every theme – food, water, fish, genetic knowledge, the purpose of farming – everything hinges on the idea of *koinonia*, on what is due to humans in common, as a result of their common right to the gift of creation, and on what is due to the rest of creation. The issue is not academic. The fate of whole communities and cultures, and indeed possibly of the whole planet, depends on it.

Ecology and the common treasury

The Stoic–Christian idea of *koinonia* already implied that the universe had to be understood as a totality. It is in the profoundest sense an ecological idea. The interconnectedness of all things is already implicit in the Priestly account of creation (Genesis 1) with its carefully integrated steps leading up to the creation of human beings and the institution of the sabbath. It is equally implicit in Paul's summary of his argument in Romans 8, where the resurrection of Christ is a promise not just to human beings but to the whole creation, groaning in bondage. For the whole of the Christian scriptures the God of history is also creator. The Noachic covenant of Genesis 8, which is the prelude to the various covenants with Israel, includes the whole of creation:

> As long as the earth endures,
> Seedtime and harvest, cold and heat,
> Summer and winter, day and night,
> Shall not cease.

> (Genesis 8.22)

Barry Commoner's well-known 'laws of ecology' are really an expression of this view. They are that everything is connected to everything else; everything must go somewhere; nature knows best; and there is no such thing as a free lunch.

That everything is connected to everything else is an apt expression of the community of creation as Paul describes it in Romans 8, where humankind is representative of the whole created order 'groaning in travail'. We exist as part of a web of relationships in which everything affects everything else. This means that, although it is important to insist against the socio-biologists that with human beings evolution becomes history, nevertheless 'nature' and history are bound up together. Adam Smith already recognized this. In the same book in which he extolled the working of self-interest he noted that 'Man ought to regard himself, not as something separated and detached, but as a citizen of the world, a member of the vast common-wealth of nature and to the interest of this great community, he ought at all times be willing that his own little interest be sacrificed.' This part of his teaching never gained the fame of his earlier observation.

That 'nature knows best' is one way of putting the basic thesis of natural law that we may deduce what is right from observing how nature works. Again, in the light of the claim that nature is red in tooth and claw, we may feel this is a very dubious nostrum. 'Nature', we can say, is a human construc-tion and may be read in very different ways. This is true, but it is surely significant that when Germany's legal system had to be reconstructed at the end of World War II jurists turned to natural law, the notion of things which were true, right and obvious 'by nature', which included all the basic freedoms of the United Nations Declaration of Human Rights. In terms of agriculture it can be rephrased, in Colin Tudge's terms, as a way of saying that 'biology will not be brooked'. We cannot simply do as we will with the natural world, and the attempt to do so invariably leads to disaster. The idea that nature knows best calls for a proper humility in our practice.

That everything must go somewhere and that there is no such thing as a free lunch are both ways of saying that everything has consequences. The conceit that economics was a 'pure science', and that it could be conducted though mathematical modelling, led it to overlook this obvious point, an oversight with dire consequences.

Knowing when to stop

Christianity learned from Stoicism but it modified it drastically, above all in reading the whole story of creation in the light of a particular life and death, that of Jesus of Nazareth. A key thing it took from that story was an account of the significance of human sin. In Paul's writings sin is a 'power' under which we are 'bound'. The question is not primarily of the extraordinary viciousness, wickedness or even selfishness of particular human beings, but of the way in which we all collectively get trapped in life-denying forms of behaviour. A good example of this is the way in which human beings can destroy the complex ecological balance which sustains them. The economist E. F. Schumacher argued that, 'Nature always . . . knows when to stop. Greater even than the mystery of natural growth is the mystery of the natural cessation of growth . . . the system of nature, of which man is part, tends to be self-balancing, self-adjusting, self-cleansing'.

Human beings, unfortunately, do not know when to stop – a prime complaint of ancient moralists, including the Church Fathers already cited. On the individual level this is the stuff of tragedy – think of Macbeth! – but it has a collective dimension as well. All over the ancient near east civilizations eliminated themselves by overfarming and overgrazing, and turning their hinterlands into desert. Humans are themselves part of nature but modify natural processes in uniquely constructive or destructive ways. Constructive intervention has found ways to grow more and better vegetables, grains and fruit, to use animals which can process cellulose to produce a huge range of dairy products, to irrigate in ways which sustain populations over millennia, as in Egypt. Destructive intervention, on the other hand, can produce terminator seeds, put fertile land under tarmac, overirrigate so that salinization makes land unproductive, fell trees so that desert takes over, in short, destroy a host ecological system as in ancient Sumeria.

The need to know when to stop has an especial significance in a world dedicated to consumption, with unparalleled means of chasing its wants. If everyone in the world lived at the level of the one fifth of the world who belong to the world's consumer class, we would need another three planets. Currently we are in denial, and the idea that technology will do the job is a prime example of that. Herman Daly estimates that environmental performance would need to improve technological performance twentyfold simply to stabilize at current rates of global pollution; and Kyoto recognized the need to urgently reduce that. General Motors undertook to have an alternative to the internal combustion engine on the road by 2002. So far no convincing alternative is in the offing.

The tragedy of the commons

The potential for humans to destroy their environment was noted in a celebrated, or notorious, article by Garret Hardin on 'the tragedy of the commons'. His view is precisely that of John Dyer: 'In fields promiscuous held, all culture languishes'. Given a common grazing area and a number of farmers, he argued, each farmer will be led by self-interest to overgraze and the result will be the destruction of the commons. 'Each man is locked into a system that compels him to increase his herd

11

without limit – in a world that is limited. Ruin is the destination toward which all men rush, each pursuing his own best interest in a society that believes in the freedom of the commons. Freedom in a commons brings ruin to all'.

The ruin of the commons followed, Hardin argued, from Adam Smith's assumption that the result of everyone following their self-interest will be mutual benefit. In fact, he argued, it is quite the contrary. We need by law, therefore, to make quite clear that some things are not 'common'. The privatization of land, in his view, was what saved it from destruction, and looking at the North American National Parks he foresaw the need to restrict visitors in some way if their beauty was to be retained.

Interestingly, while there are clear examples of the tragedy of the commons, as we shall see, Hardin's original example was not best chosen to make his point. The old English commons were not overgrazed, but this was because each person with a right to them zealously policed his neighbour. It was bonds of community, the need to survive in a community with a strong common ethos, which prevented overgrazing. Hardin's selfish commoner would have been literally or metaphorically pilloried. Rather than the inefficacy of conscience being the root of the problem, as Hardin suggests, it is the absence of real community which leads to the tragedy he outlined. The question, then, is what 'real community' might mean in the global village, and a cogent suggestion is some version of the United Nations. As I write, in 2005, the irony is that the US is systematically undoing 60 years of work in attempting to build this community in every area, from trade to pollution to human rights, in the interests of its own hubristically imperialist claims.

Hardin's preferred solution to the tragedy of the commons, private ownership, makes clear that his assumptions do not include the idea of the common treasury. Later on, in another parable, he suggested the idea of lifeboat ethics, an idea which quite literally goes back to the ark! Hardin modifies the image: there is a plimsoll line on the ark, and we have overloaded it. When the boat goes down we take to the liferafts, but there is not room for all. Only some – implicitly the rich in North America – will be left to inherit the earth. Hardin's neo-Malthusian views have from the start attracted the accusation of racism. The Church Fathers would say that the more fundamental problem is the idea of private ownership. Long before Gandhi, Basil of Caesarea noted that there was enough for everyone's need, but not for everyone's greed. 'If each one would take that which is sufficient for one's needs', he wrote, 'leaving what is in excess to those in distress, no one would be rich, no one poor'. The question, in other words, is about justice. For the Church Fathers, the problem arises precisely when we abandon the idea of the common treasury.

Ecosystem justice

In scripture the central term for justice is 'shalom', the situation of peace with justice which follows from following the provisions of YHWH's covenant. Shalom is what today we call 'ecosytem justice', which goes beyond, though it includes, distributive justice. Distributive justice is certainly essential. That more than 840 million people go hungry in a world where food is dumped at less than the cost of production and land is set aside is obviously due to a failure of such justice, and not to the fact that there is insufficient to go round. This injustice has to be addressed, but in itself it is inadequate. Justice as shalom embraces every aspect of creation, and focuses on relationships between the interdependent parts. In scripture it is bound up with the idea of rest. The Priestly account of creation, it has long been noted, does not culminate with the creation of men and women, but with the sabbath rest. God rests from God's labours and human beings are invited to share that rest. The weekly sabbath shocked the Roman historian Tacitus, who complained about the weekly strike observed by Jews. Israel had long since extended it both to the land and to animals. Just as debts were to be remitted every seven years, according to Deuteronomy so, too, the land had to be given rest. According to Leviticus the sabbath rest had to include slaves and the animals. Behind these pieces of legislation lie complex perceptions both about the nature of human life, but also about God's intentions for creation. Shalom, peace and justice, includes rest, a day off. The point is that life is more than labour. Humans are not, as they were in the Babylonian epics, simply slaves of the gods. By the same token, no created thing is there simply to be exploited. In virtue of its creation it had its own dignity, its own entitlement to rest, and to ignore that was both folly and sin.

Lewis Mumford spoke of the change from an ethic of conservation to a view of the world based on extraction, on mining. In his view this happened some time in the sixteenth century. The fundamental metaphor for the world ceased to be that of a garden, or a farm, and became that of a mine, which you exploited until its resources ran out before moving on. The idea that resources might some day run out simply did not occur. Given the likely world population of, say 1550, and given the technology available, that was not so stupid an assumption, but as technology became more successful it became more and more dangerous. As we shall see in Chapter 5, the idea that Christianity is to blame for the ecological crisis in virtue of its use of the 'domination text' (Genesis 1.28) is highly simplistic, but domination became more and more the approach to natural resources and in some circles, particularly around the oil industry, remains so. Once full-scale industrialization was in place it became a rule that the wheels must never cease turning: it was 'inefficient' for them to do so. The world's economy was predicated not on a rhythm of production and rest, but on endless production and consumption. As our ancestors sowed, so are we reaping. Climate changes experienced now are the product of human behaviour up to 50 years ago. What we are currently storing up for our descendants can only be guessed.

The biosphere as part of the commons

Although Hardin's principal concern was population he presciently pointed to pollution as part of the problem he outlined. Today the most serious problem to do with the commons is the assault on the biosphere which sustains all life. This biosphere is the most fundamental aspect of the commons, a fact recognized by organizations like the Global Commons Institute, which campaigns to reduce carbon dioxide emissions. The biosphere is a cycle in which 'every plant yielding seed', as Genesis puts it, transforms carbon dioxide, produces oxygen during photosynthesis and in turn uses up oxygen and releases carbon dioxide. This cycle has been disrupted in the past 200 years by colossal manmade discharges of carbon dioxide, as well as the other greenhouse gases – methane, nitrous oxide and CFCs. According to the Intergovernmental Panel on Climate Change (IPCC) the present carbon dioxide concentration has not been exceeded during the past 420,000 years and probably not during the past 20 million years. Currently we are adding six billion tons of carbon to the atmosphere each year. The result is a hotter planet. Enthusiasts for the market economy who concede that global warming is occurring sometimes suggest that warmer temperatures do not matter as we will all live in the equivalent of California. This is to fail to recognize the ecological nature of reality: that everything we do has effects for good or ill. We are already seeing damaging results from global warming but even more fundamentally all life on earth, and not just human life, thrives within a relatively narrow temperature band. The addition of just one degree may dramatically raise the level of species extinction, and a few degrees could lead to irreversible damage. A 'business as usual' agenda could put all life out of business.

The impacts of global warming are at least sixfold. In no particular order they include desertification in various parts of the world, but especially in China where 2,500 kilometres turns to desert each year. According to the Food and Agriculture Organization (FAO), 250 million people have been directly affected by the spread of deserts and another billion are at risk. Water supply is also affected. The melting of glaciers in the Himalayas, the Andes and the Alps puts millions of people at risk by the potential failure of water supply. At the same time rising sea levels put populations in the Pacific, China, Bangladesh, Egypt and Nigeria at risk. In Britain the Flood Defence Agency is preparing for this sea level rise on the east coast. Pacific islands are already disappearing. On the World Council of Churches (WCC) website a plaintive appeal from the Solomon Islands reads: 'We do not want your aid; we do not even want fairer trade; we just want you to change your lifestyles'. The depletion of the ozone layer caused by the release of CFCs may also lead to the loss of plankton in turn reducing their ability to remove carbon dioxide from the atmosphere and so advancing global warming.

Climate change

As many of us are experiencing, climate change means the prevalence of more severe weather, with sharp swings between wet and dry, hot and cold. When El Nīno hit Honduras the country's president said they lost in 72 hours what it had taken

50 years to build. The damage done by Hurricane Katrina will take years to repair according to US sources. Again, tropical diseases will spread northwards and agricultural pests and diseases will no longer be checked by harsh winters – assuming, that is, that the Arctic melt does not put the Gulf Stream into reverse and introduce an arctic climate into Britain. If that happened the equator would simultaneously get hotter and food supply would become the most pressing world issue. How even the present population could be fed would be a major problem. A report in September 2005 suggests that the Arctic could be ice-free before the end of the present century. A Colorado scientist notes that 'Feedbacks in the system are starting to take hold. We could see changes in Arctic ice happening much sooner than we thought'. The results of such changes are unpredictable. At worst whole ecosystems could unravel, something which is already beginning to happen in Alaska, where the greenhouse effect is amplified by the positive feedback of sun on ice. There has been a rise of six degrees centigrade in wintertime temperatures there. Bizarrely, in the summer of 2005 more than 150,000 tourists flew up to see these changes for themselves. Here in Alaska the journalist Mark Lynas records some of the greatest hostility to Greenpeace and anyone concerned with ecology, on the grounds that such concern threatens oil jobs.

Such hostility is found at the highest levels of the United States administration. In 2005 the Chair of the House of Representatives committee on energy and commerce, with close links to the oil industry, called in all the material ever published by the leading climate scientists alleging flaws in the research. He has been accused of a McCarthyite witch hunt in which political review is being substituted for peer review. The Pentagon, however, has taken climate change seriously. In its forward planning it takes into account the probability that climate change could lead to anarchy as countries develop a nuclear threat to defend and secure dwindling food and energy supplies. And as of August 2005 senators with an eye on the White House are visiting Alaska and at least thinking about how climate change might be tackled.

Why is global warming happening? Those who deny that 'the science' represented by the IPCC can be trusted refer to previous ice ages and periods of drought as evidence that there is a climate cycle which the earth goes through. Climate change would thus be outside our control and have to be accepted as fate. Beliefs such as this, supported by scientists payrolled by the oil industry, have meant that no action has been taken in the 35 years since climate change was first put on the agenda by the Club of Rome. If we accept the IPCC argument that climate change is caused by human activity, however, what specifically is driving it? We can give a number of answers to that question.

Of course the doubling of the world's population since 1950 is a major part of the problem, but the key thing is that this has happened in a world committed to relentless growth. The International Monetary Fund (IMF) insists on growth at four per cent per annum, while China, the world's largest population, is growing at ten per cent a year. A globally competitive economy means that every firm and every country has to grow in relation to its competitor or it will lose out. When firms announce their annual or even half-yearly profits a return of billions will not satisfy shareholders if it is a few billions less than last year. This need to grow locks the whole world into a suicidal spiral. The claim of the World Trade Organization (WTO) that economic growth is good for the environment because it shares around cleaner technologies is ludicrous, as the staggering rise in food miles ought to tell us.

Economic activity, in turn, shapes political decisions. The US accounts for one quarter of the world's greenhouse effects but has only four per cent of its population. At Rio in 1992 George

Bush senior famously announced that 'the American way of life is non-negotiable'. His son reiterated that he would not accept anything that would harm the American economy or American workers, a major reason why the US will not sign up to Kyoto, as it considers that concessions to majority world countries would give them an unfair advantage. This is Hardin's tragedy of the commons with a vengeance, global anarchy far more dangerous than terrorism, as the Canadian Environment Minister has complained.

Corporations

Behind the politicians stand the corporations which gave millions of dollars to get Bush re-elected and who, on both sides of the Atlantic, lobby for more relaxed regulation of industry. In the US government inspections have been nearly halved since 1998. The present system relies on the goodwill of corporations to report their emissions honestly and, as the Enron corporation shows, it is a delusion to think that corporations will act in any other way than to maximize profits. On the contrary, corporate criminologist Paul Braithwaite found, after an examination of the Fortune 500 top firms, that capitalism was 'intrinsically criminogenic' and that all of them, in one way or another, had been involved in criminal activity. With regard to polluting activities what this means is that Hardin's 'tragedy of the commons' is played out.

Meanwhile, as Susan George has noted, many of the world's most heavily indebted countries include those which have the largest forests, needed for the recycling of carbon dioxide. IMF policies have meant that these countries have needed to sell hardwood, or to raze forests in order to make room for cash-crop production or for beef-ranching. Deforestation and land-use changes are responsible for at least 20 per cent of annual carbon dioxide emissions.

Consumers

The fault does not just lie in the hands of corporations and governments. Most of those who live in the so-called 'developed' world are part of it. In so far as we are consumers we play our part. The US and the European Union with only ten per cent of the world's population are responsible for 45 per cent of all carbon dioxide emissions. Texas emits more than France and California more than Brazil. UK per capita emissions total 9.6 tonnes of carbon dioxide a year, where a sustainable person's is 2.45 tonnes. Transport is the fastest growing contributor to global warming and, quite apart from haulage, 89 per cent of people say they would find it very hard to live without cars and when the British government tried to raise petrol taxes (admittedly already the highest in Europe) they quickly had to back down in the face of fuel protests. In Britain and North America, meanwhile, people are hooked on short flights, increasingly using them not just for holidays but for journeys even within small countries like Britain. A single short-haul flight produces as much carbon dioxide as the average motorist does in a year.

The tragedy of the commons is apparent in the reactions this evokes. Not unnaturally India and China, whose citizens emit only a tenth and a quarter as much as the average British citizen, ask why they should limit their emissions when all they are doing is to reach the point we have reached now. The Global Commons Institute proposes plans for 'contraction and convergence' according to which developing countries are allowed to increase their emissions for a time, while developed countries decrease theirs, with a view to a common reduction in the next century. The question, of course, is whether we have enough time for such plans and whether it is feasible that eight or ten billion people can live at the level that is now taken for granted in the West. It is that question which is exercising the Pentagon. Back in 1948 the US policy planner George Kennan noted:

> We [i.e. America] have fifty per cent of the world's wealth but only 6.3 per cent of its population . . . In this situation we cannot fail to be the object of envy and resentment . . . Our real task in the coming period is to devise a pattern of relationships which will allow us to maintain this position of disparity. We should cease to talk about the raising of living standards, human rights and democratisation. The day is not far off when we are going to have to deal in straight power concepts. The less we are then hampered by idealistic slogans the better.

To apply this view to global warming is to take the view that, come what may, you will preserve a lifestyle premised on cheap oil even if you have to take the whole world with you.

Technological fixes

The present response to these problems is to insist that it is possible to have one's cake and eat it. Just after the G8 summit at Gleneagles in July 2005 the US hosted a meeting for some of the big players (India, China and Australia) to find ways of dealing with climate change through technological fixes. Other countries seek to deal with it by 'offsets'. Thus Tony Blair announced that the G8 summit would be carbon neutral by dint of tree-planting elsewhere in the world. But in the first place some of these schemes, like the planting of a huge eucalyptus plantation in Brazil, have an enormous negative impact on biodiversity, and pollute and reduce the surrounding water sources. More seriously, as Heidi Bachram notes, scientific understanding of the complex interactions between the biosphere (trees, oceans, etc.) and the troposphere (the lowermost part of the atmosphere) is limited. She comments: 'There is no scientific credibility for the practice of soaking up pollution using tree plantations.' In Britain the House of Commons Environmental Audit Committee noted that the focus on climate science and technology 'is creating the appearance of activity . . . whilst evading the harder national and international political decisions which must be made if there is to be a solution'. The Global Commons Institute is of the view that these ploys tackle neither rising emissions nor atmospheric greenhouse gas concentrations. They fail to recognize that climate change is a justice issue, in that the richest 20 per cent of the world's population uses nearly 60 per cent of all energy.

Emissions quotas

Another scheme, proposed by Kyoto, was trading in emissions quotas. Thus underperforming economies, like that of Russia, can sell their polluting rights to countries who are over-performing. Analogously, the UK government has devised a scheme whereby an oil platform in a less sensitive ecological area can sell credits to an operation in an extremely sensitive area and continue to do harm. Both schemes are predicated first on the idea that we can continue business as usual, and second that problems can be dealt with by market mechanisms. The Durban Declaration on Carbon Trading notes that the attempt to trade in carbon follows the reduction of everything else to a commodity and that the Earth's ability and capacity to support a climate conducive to life and human societies is now passing into the same corporate hands that are destroying the climate. Tom Burke, of Imperial College, London, puts it still more robustly, describing the attempt to apply cost benefit analysis to climate change as 'junk economics'. 'It is a vanity of economists', he writes, 'to believe that all choices can be boiled down to calculations of monetary value'.

In Britain the green rhetoric of the government escalates, but so do the tax cuts given to the oil industry, the promotion of air travel, building more roads and, in the UK, houses and public buildings which only meet minimum environmental audits. In John Prescott's drive for four million new homes sustainability is not high on the agenda. On the part of governments the failure to act is driven by fear of taking decisions which might cost an election in four years' time. On the part of the populations they govern it is denial, a refusal to contemplate anything which might interfere with the hedonist lifestyle to which we have become accustomed. Hardin argues that natural selection favours the forces of psychological denial. The individual benefits from his ability to deny the truth even though society as a whole suffers. The tragedy of the commons is then written into our evolutionary history. Against this is Aristotle's view that humans differ from other animals in making rather than inheriting their political and economic systems. He advanced this idea in one of human history's greatest treatises on ethics, politics and economics.

With human beings, an Aristotelian or Thomist would argue, evolution becomes history and we can shape it as we please, though of course this involves struggle. Hardin believes that the preservation of food production was ensured by private property, but that the tragedy of the commons as a cesspool had to be prevented by coercive laws or taxing devices that make it cheaper for the polluter to treat his pollutants than to discharge them untreated. That this will involve struggle can be seen on a small scale by the threat of fuel protests whenever the price of petrol gets too high. Even more dangerously, neither governments nor corporations will compromise either standard of living or profits. Nothing, it seems, will be conceded willingly. The final document of the World Council of Churches' Consultation in Seoul proclaimed:

> We will resist the claim that anything in creation is merely a resource for human exploitation. We will resist species extinction

for human benefit; consumerism and harmful mass production; pollution of land, air and waters; all human activities which are now leading to probable rapid climate change; and policies which contribute to the disintegration of creation.

That resistance is today's political imperative and it calls for an even bigger paradigm change than that at the end of the nineteenth century which gave us our current liberal democratic parties. In their rapturous embrace of the market all these parties fail us. If we are to survive we need to find a more responsible democratic alternative. The matter is urgent. According to the consultation on climate change held in South Africa in October 2005 the world community has five years in which to act before the negative effects of climate change become irreversible.

I have argued that economic activity is at the heart of the problem of misuse of the commons, and that this is a key issue if we are to think meaningfully about harvest. Accordingly I turn in the next chapter to look more closely at issues of trade and the forces which are driving the present movement of enclosure.

For further reflection and action

- How, as a church and as individuals, can we promote a situation where every person lives 'under their vine and fig tree'?
- What is the ecological footprint of our church? Of our home? Of our community?
- If we have five years before the damaging consequences of climate change become irreversible how ought we to change our lifestyles?
- What changes would we like to see adopted by our government?

2

Power games

The gospel of the market

The common treasury is, as we saw in the last chapter, an eco-logical idea, but it is also an expression of social justice. The earth is held in common on the basis of the fundamental equal-ity of all persons. The economic system for which Locke was already giving a rationale, however, turns the common treasury into the playground or theatre of a competitive power game. The fundamental principles of the contemporary economic system were classically laid down by Adam Smith in 1776. Smith was a rationalist, a friend of David Hume, and in *The Wealth of Nations* he effectively rewrites the theology in which he had been brought up. As a child he had learned that 'man's chief end is to worship God and to glorify him for ever'. In his moral philosophy he had defined human beings in terms of sympathy but here, more momentously, he notes 'a natural propensity to barter, truck and exchange one thing for another'. He does not, of course, say that this is the only thing human beings do but, as economics gained a more and more impor-tant role in political life, and separated from moral philosophy, this came to be the implication. It is a fundamentally different starting point from Aristotle for whom human beings are dis-tinguished from animals by the gift of reason which they have in order to shape their community, a definition which came into the Christian bloodstream through Aquinas. From being homo sapiens we become homo mercator, trading beings. Not yet 30 years after the publication of Smith's book William Wordsworth understood:

> How dire a thing
> Is worshipped in that idol proudly named
> 'The Wealth of Nations'.

Smith had also learned at school that 'God overrules all things for perfectly wise and loving ends'. In his account of the hidden hand he redefines both providence and ethics. Smith argued that markets, left to themselves, tend to fix prices at their proper and just rate. Picking up the scholastic doctrine of the just price he argued that supply and demand even the market out towards what he called the 'natural price'. In his view markets tend toward equilibrium, in which output of a commodity equals demand. Justice, then, is whatever turns out to be the outcome of the market.

In his discussion of economics Aquinas turns from trade to justice, and decides what is and is not possible by the standards of the latter. Smith, however, opens the gate for those like Hayek who define justice simply in terms of what the market produces. Naively, Smith argued that capital, when accrued, tends to be used for the purposes most beneficial to society. The best thing government can do, therefore, is to keep out of things – simply to provide the framework for trade. Today this is a key part of the dogma of the Washington consensus, the new economic orthodoxy. The present neo-liberal doctrine that the role of the state is to provide a secure environment for transnational investment and competition, and that the principal responsibility of government is investor security, is the bastard child of Smith's view.

Another gospel

The redefinition of human nature, providence and ethics makes it easier to understand how this account of the 'economy' is presented as a gospel, an article of faith, defended as fiercely, and with as little attention to reality, as the faith of the most crazed fanatic. In this context, theologically, we have to heed Paul's warning to the Galatians: 'If anyone proclaims to you a gospel contrary to the one you received let them be accursed' (Galatians 1.9). The claims of the free market to constitute the human good, to be the narrative of the world, constitute another gospel, a gospel which defines human progress in terms of consumption and which is driving the ecological crisis. It is, moreover, claimed to be a gospel written into the very structure of the universe. The claim that there is no alternative to the market rests on a neo-Darwinian construal of Smith's appeal to self-interest. We are all 'rational utility maximizers' we are told, all the way down, and this fact determines what is and is not possible politically and socially. This total claim on our being demands a theological challenge.

Redefining economics

A first step in challenging this pseudo-gospel is to broaden what we understand by economics. The word derives from the Greek word *oikonomia*, household management. We find it in Luke's story of the unjust *oikonomos*, translated as 'steward' in the AV, but meaning 'a manager of a household' (which is not to justify recent translations of *oikonomos* as 'manager'). In this sense we are all economists. We can be either just or unjust stewards. To be an economist is to manage our affairs in such a way as to further what we perceive to be good ends. It involves a moral judgement. This was recognized by the inclusion of economics as a part of moral philosophy from Aristotle to John Maynard Keynes who, in his *General Theory*, still speaks of economics as a branch of moral enquiry. 'Economists', then, are not just people who advise governments or the World Bank or teach in economics departments at universities. We are all economists, but we must distinguish levels of involvement.

The initial level implied in the Greek word is that of the *domestic economy*: the level which is of concern to all of us all of our lives and with which we are most familiar. How to balance expenditure, roughly, against income. That activity draws on the *local economy:* the shops where I buy my food, the real ale establishments I patronize, the clubs or theatres, or sporting venues I attend. The local economy in turn relates to the *regional*, and that to the *national*. This is what the Chancellor of the Exchequer draws up his plans about, and involves trying to meet myriad demands within the budget allowed by the productive activity of the citizenry. Beyond that, however, comes what we have become increasingly familiar with over the past 30 years – the *global economy* – the intermeshing of the regional and national economies of the whole world, so that in some sense my shopping is dependent upon the labour of unknown millions in the remotest parts of the world.

All these levels of the economy are absolutely familiar. What you never read in the newspapers, however, and what very few professional economists seem to realize, is that all these levels of economic activity are dependent upon what the Kentucky farmer and philosopher Wendell Berry calls 'the great economy'. The great economy is the giftedness of all reality, our ultimate dependence on photosynthesis, the fact that we do not, and cannot – not even with the most advanced genetic science – create the raw materials of life out of nothing. The great economy, theologically God's creation of all things, or grace,

sustains all that is. We are part of it, bound up in the bundle
of life with the slugs which eat our lettuces, with the oil we
extract and on which we cravenly depend, and with each other.
In that sense it is quite wrong to speak, as people sometimes
still do, of an 'environmental problem'. We are part of the
whole. Our peculiarity as humans is in our capacity for creative
management on the one hand, and our capacity for damage on
the other.

This layering of economic activity means that 'economics' is
a far bigger thing than is represented in the 'economics' or
'financial' pages of the newspapers. It is far bigger than what is
dealt with by the Chancellor of the Exchequer. Economics is the
management of the whole *oikoumene*, to use another, and related, Greek word, the whole inhabited earth, in the interests of
fullness of life (John 10.10). To evaluate our economic activity
is to evaluate what we are doing in relation to that goal.

Lewis Mumford suggested that human economic activity, in
this very large sense, can be configured in five different ways.
There was, first, a *primeval phase* in which human populations
differed little from other omnivorous mammals. As hunter-
gatherers humans lived for 350,000 generations. This was
followed by the *early farming phase* beginning around 12,000
years ago. Spreading domestication and advancing farming
techniques led to humankind beginning to change the face of
the earth. This in turn was followed by the *early urban phase*
5,000 years ago, first in Mesopotamia and then India and
China. Occupational specialization gathered pace creating
more permanent divides in society. More productive agriculture led to surpluses which could support growing cities, and so
all over the world, prosperous cities arose wherever they could
draw on rural hinterlands. This phase, in which most of the
population worked in peasant agriculture, and a small proportion lived and worked in cities, accounts for most of what

we call 'history'. The fourth, *urban industrial phase* began in Europe about 200 years ago. It was associated with a major mechanization of production and massive increases in energy consumption both overall and per capita. It delivered huge improvements in sanitation, health and education, and eventually in housing. Population began to shift to the cities and at the same time to grow rapidly. Historians guess that world population may have been 350 million in 1650. Britain in 1700 may have had a population of just over two million. By 1801, the date of the first census, it was 11 million; by 1901, 33 million and by 2001 60 million. World population had soared to three billion by 1950. Even at that late date, the majority of human beings still lived in villages. The fifth phase, in which we now live, is the *global interdependence phase* in which cities act as nodal points of unprecedented flows of resources, wastes, traded products and services, finance capital and labour. It has seen human population double in just over 50 years to more than six billion and within the last five years the number of people living in cities has finally passed the 50 per cent mark.

The last two phases of human development have generated every benefit we currently take for granted, at the top of which are adequate diet and shelter, good dentistry, good medicine, and effective contraception. If you doubt these gains, read Dorothy Wordsworth's *Diary*, or C. R. Leslie's *Memoirs of Constable*. Even for middle-class people, these documents make clear, death and disease were constant terrors, while Cobbet's *Rural Rides*, from the same period, paints a grim picture of rural poverty, starvation and atrocious housing. That world was still around in Britain, in part, until after World War II. Food rationing remained in place until 1954. By 1959, however, Harold Macmillan could tell us, 'You never had it so good', and he was right. Standards of health, diet and housing all rose exponentially. It is these changes which account for the gospel of the free market. One can understand exactly why the gospel has so many believers. For many (though even today not for the majority of the world's citizens) it has delivered us a fantastic, hedonist society. The question is, at what cost?

Questioning the free-trade gospel

In one way or another all the problems of the market gospel stem from a failure to think ecologically, to realize that financial and industrial activity has effects, that, in Barry Commoner's words, everything is connected to everything else and there is no such thing as a free lunch. Karl Marx learned from and built upon Adam Smith's work and when he called his great study 'Capital' he meant primarily financial capital, the accruing of wealth which made industrial and agricultural expansion possible. In his study of Equality R. H. Tawney already speaks of 'social capital', the partly written but more importantly unwritten norms and attitudes which allow society to function smoothly. To use this financial metaphor, if social capital is exhausted then you have a society where nobody trusts anyone else and therefore where no communal enterprise can flourish. Ultimately societies without trust die – one of the fundamental reasons for the collapse of Stalinism. Again, very importantly, there is natural capital, the raw material of the earth without which we cannot live. A desert, we might say, would represent near bankruptcy in terms of natural capital. What comprises riches is water, waste recycling, soil formation, climate regulation, carbon sequestration, pollination and so forth. We can also think of cultural and even spiritual capital, resources without which societies cannot survive.

Beguiled by the model of trade Smith, and the free traders who followed him, ignored the problem of what today are called 'externalities' – the unintended side-effects of economic

31

action. These impinge on all the other forms of capital. In the first place there are problems such as acid rain, pollution and climate change, the direct consequence of economic activity. The word 'economic' is used to mean that something is efficient and cheap. If I have an economic car it does a relatively large number of miles to the gallon. But what counts as economic is measured purely by account books, which give us our favourite metaphor of 'the bottom line'. Thus railway lines are axed because they are 'uneconomic' – meaning that fares charged do not cover the cost of running them. Traffic is pushed onto roads because costs are then dispersed on many millions of individuals. The externalities of these decisions, their impact on the ecology, on natural capital, are not taken into account. As soon as we do that we have a very different account of what is truly economic. 'Efficiency', in the market paradigm, is judged by what makes money, but that is a suicidal strategy in a world which depends on natural capital. This is the point of the Midas parable. Midas had the gift of turning everything into gold, but this included his food, and so he died.

Again, 'economic' thinking corrodes social capital. Company chairmen prove their worth by cutting their workforces. A good company is lean and mean. The former head of Enron said it was important to get rid of people, because they gum up the works. People cost money, and therefore eat into profits. But such policies destroy social capital. Smith thought of the market as a benign providence. He and his followers, right up to the present, do not see that leaving things to 'the market' (i.e. privileging those with money) will mean that the rich will use more than their rightful share of ecosystem resources, that child soldiers will be armed around the world, that the basic needs of the poor will not be put before those of the rich and that the earth's ecosystem will be destroyed. The market fails to value either natural or social capital and thus pollutes or destroys the environment and allows communities to disintegrate. The speculator George Soros, having milked national currencies for years, now fears that the spread of market values into all areas of life is endangering democracy since open societies depend upon values which markets cannot instil, and which they actively destroy in their single-minded prioritization of profit.

The gospel of the free market has operated on the understanding that there is such a thing as a free lunch. There is no such thing and sooner or later we, or our children, will have to pay. Neo-liberal economics is essentially kamikaze economics: it hurls itself into destruction, something which the nihilism of Hayek's writing makes quite clear. The warning of the prophets, that the fathers have eaten sour grapes and the children's teeth are set on edge, is true of the generations since Smith as they have been true of no other generations. We have sown the wind and we are reaping (sometimes literally) the whirlwind.

From industrial to finance capital

The present neo-liberal economic phase in which we are living is characterized by the dominance of finance capital, the rise to power of great corporations, and the reconstruction of the world economic order by the Bretton Woods Institutions, and especially the WTO, in the interests of the corporations. I shall take these issues in turn.

The meaning of money

Under both mercantile and industrial capitalism the amount of money in circulation correlated, more or less, to goods produced. Money was a means of exchange for these goods. This fact was signified by the gold standard, which guaranteed people an equivalence between a certain number of notes and a set quantity of gold, itself a (highly fetishistic) product. David

Ricardo argued that without such an equivalence money 'would be exposed to all the fluctuations to which the ignorance of the issuers might subject it'. The second President of the US, John Adams, agreed. Every bank bill issued in excess of stocks of silver and gold, he said, 'represents nothing, and is therefore a cheat upon somebody'. He understood that in this situation money would cease to be a useful medium of exchange, a counter for real things, but become the point of the exercise. This became the situation, of course, when the dollar came off the gold standard in 1971. Two things have happened since then. First, there has been an exponential growth of the debt economy. Money has been created, not in response to productive activity, but to fuel consumer spending on mortgages, personal loans and overdrafts. Modern money is, says Michael Rowbotham, entirely abstract and empty of meaning. What is called the 'money supply' is a spiral of loans built upon loans: 'This empty spiral of numbers based upon numbers is the heart of the financial system upon which economies throughout the entire world are built'. It is scarcely surprising that a former director of the Bank of England, Lord Josiah Stamp, should have written:

> The modern banking system manufactures money out of nothing. The process is perhaps the most astounding piece of sleight of hand that was ever invented. Banking was conceived in iniquity and born in sin. Bankers own the earth; take it away from them, but leave them with the power to create credit, and with a stroke of a pen they will create enough money to buy it back again . . . If you want to be slaves of the bankers, and pay the costs of your own slavery, then let the banks create money.

A confidence trick

If you described the process as a confidence trick you would not be being abusive, but precise. Confidence is at the heart of the whole process. It is clear in George Soros' betting on the pound or the mark, which created a crisis of confidence in those currencies. He caused the devaluation of the mark first by placing bets against it, and then by publishing a letter in *The Times* saying that he expected it to fall against other currencies. It did so. As opposed to the world of industrial capital the new world of finance capital represents precisely this kind of speculation. Nearly two billion dollars are exchanged on the currency markets every day but they do not correspond to anything real. When the stock market crashed the world was not poorer by a single item. The global stock market functions as a gigantic casino in which astronomic fortunes can be made or lost and which dominates the global economy to the detriment of what is truly productive.

The kind of behaviour this leads to is exemplified by a report in the *Financial Times* in October 2000 concerning the settlement of a dispute between a New York hedge fund and the government of Peru, settled in favour of the former. Elliott Associates bought defaulted bank loans at half their face value and then insisted on reclaiming them at their full value. US courts awarded the fund $58 million – money transferred directly from the poor of Peru to the rich in New York. Jubilee 2000, an organization campaigning for debt relief, commented: 'These people are trading in human misery. Elliott Associates are picking over the bones of the Peruvian economy like a pack of vultures. It may be just business to them but to the children of Peru it is school books, medicines and clean water'. Elliott also targeted Ecuador, the Ivory Coast, Panama, Poland and Congo. Such behaviour is the reality of globalization, the true nature of the global market.

The growth of corporate power

It is this world which underpins corporate trade. Unlike in Smith's day it is corporations that trade rather than nations, and corporations which set the terms of trade. Corporations account for a staggering 70 per cent of all trade conducted around the world. A third of world wide exports are intra-firm movements. Three hundred corporations own one quarter of world productive assets and half of the 100 largest economies in the world are corporations. The largest ten corporations have three times the total income of the world's poorest countries and yet at the same time the top 200, which conduct almost a third of the entire planet's economic activity, employ less than one quarter of one per cent of the world's workforce. Meanwhile the least developed countries, with ten per cent of the world's population, have 0.3 per cent of world trade, half their share of 20 years ago. These developments would have horrified Adam Smith. 'The capricious ambition of kings and ministers', he wrote, 'has not been more fatal to the repose of Europe than the impertinent jealousy of merchants and manufactures'. Merchants and manufacturers, in his view, were not supposed to be the rulers of humanity, and he believed it was the function of government to see that they should not be. This is another part of Smith's doctrine which has been conveniently overlooked in present neo-liberal orthodoxy.

Corporations have been compared, blasphemously, to the suffering servant of Isaiah because, in the eyes of their protagonists, they exist to serve the rest of the world and are unfairly vilified in doing so. But because their goal is profit they routinely weaken labour, environmental and public health laws. They make sure that they pay tax where rates are lowest. Only three per cent of them have corporate social responsibility codes and even these are drawn up without consulting workers.

Avoiding responsibility

When things go wrong, which they frequently do, corporations hide behind the so-called 'corporate veil' which creates the legal fiction that a parent and subsidiary companies are completely separate from one another. This is what happened in India in Bhopal where 4,000 people around the Union Carbide plant died from a gas leak. Again in India, at least 12,000 children worked on farms in 2003 supplying cotton seeds to subsidiaries of agrifood corporations. The deaths of 30 children in India from the effects of pesticide spraying are being investigated. In Peru 24 children died as a result of drinking Bayer pesticides, packed without a hazard warning and labelled only in Spanish which the Quechua-speaking Indians could not read. The packets had a picture of vegetables and were taken for instant soup. Bayer has neither paid compensation nor apologized.

The hidden fist

Corporations wield enormous political power. In 2001 Vermont Congressman Bernie Sanders published an article saying that, in view of the unprecedented wealth and power of the corporations, it was imperative to launch a grassroots revolution to enable ordinary Americans to regain control of their country. After raising more money than any president in history G. W. Bush passed a bill which gave 500 billion dollars in tax breaks to the wealthiest one per cent of Americans. In 1993 when Clinton proposed that the government should offer some form of healthcare protection to the 40 million Americans who were uninsured, the insurance industry spent 100 million dollars on lobbying, 60 million dollars million on advertising and provided members of Congress with around 350 free trips to make sure this would not happen.

Unsurprisingly, government yields to this kind of persuasion. Super and Special 301 clauses of the US Trade Act allow the US to take unilateral action against any country that does not open its markets to US corporations. Super 301 forces freedom for investment; Special 301 forces freedom for monopoly control of markets through intellectual property rights protection. And the right-wing columnist Thomas Friedman notes ingenuously that 'The hidden hand of the market will never work without the hidden fist . . . and the hidden fist that keeps the world safe for Silicon Alley's technologies to flourish is called the US army, Air Force, Navy and Marine Corps'.

The possession of power is both marked and actualized by the revolving door between business and government. In the United States a multinational chemical and agricultural products attorney quit his job with the company's law firm, went to work for the Food and Drug Administration (FDA) and wrote a regulation that allowed that company's product into the food supply. Paul O'Neill, a multimillionaire who had been top executive of two of the world's largest corporations became secretary to the Treasury and proposed that corporations should be totally exempt from income tax. He also called for the abolition of Social Security, Medicaid and Medicare for working people because able-bodied adults should be able to provide for their own retirement. In Britain Lord Sainsbury serves as a government minister, and Ken Clarke speaks of what he has learned by acting as a director for firms like British Tobacco. In France the CEO of the water company Suez moves from his job into government.

Power and control

What the corporations are interested in is not simply power but outright control. Calgene, now a subsidiary of Monsanto, the California biotech company famous for its attempt to get a genetically modified tomato on the table, set out its corporate agenda thus:

> Our objective is to control production with our partners from
> the production of foundation seed to the sale of the oil to our

customers. We want complete control. The seed margins don't begin to cover the cost of investments we've made in the technology. The way you capture value added is selling oil – value-added oil at a premium to customers, period. So we and our partners will maintain complete control of the process.

Similarly, the company chairman of McDonalds said in 1994, 'Our goal is to totally dominate the quick service industry worldwide . . . I want McDonald's to be more than a leader. I want McDonald's to dominate'. 'As huge as our world of Coca-Cola is today', says an executive of that firm, 'it is just a tiny sliver of the world we can create'.

And who owns the corporations? For whom do they speak with these imperialist visions? The less than 0.7 per cent of the world's population who have any stocks and shares. Corporate chairmen are accountable to their shareholders and have a legal duty to try and make them profits, milking the global economy, therefore, for the benefit of less than one per cent of the world's richest people.

Corporate power in the agricultural sector

The power of corporations is especially clear in agriculture where vertically integrated corporations control operations 'from farm to fork', covering seeds, fertilizers, equipment, processing, transport and marketing. Market concentration is now at its highest level since records began. Speaking about the wave of mergers in the biotech industry in 1996 the vice-president of Monsanto described it as 'a consolidation of the whole food chain'. The FAO panel on ethics in food and agriculture notes that 'there are serious imbalances arising from the concentration of economic power in the hands of a few'. A few examples of this will have to suffice: six corporations handle 85 per cent of world trade in grain, eight account for up to 60 per cent of trade in coffee, seven account for 90 per cent of tea, three account for 83 per cent of cocoa, three account for 80 per cent of trade in bananas. Four big soya traders/processors control three-quarters of the US and European soya market. Six corporations control three-quarters of the global pesticides market. One company, Cargill, which is still mostly owned by the descendants of the founder, is the world's largest oil seed trader, and has major stakes in phosphate fertilizer, grain, coffee, cocoa, sugar, seeds, malt and poultry. It controls nearly half of US maize exports, a third of all soybean exports and a fifth of wheat exports. The company operates in 61 countries. Other business includes meat-processing, cotton, sugar and petroleum trading; financial trading; food processing; futures brokering; feed and fertilizer production; and steelmaking. Through its ownership of grain elevators and transport it controls 45 per cent of global grain distribution. Cargill's turnover in 2000 was 48 billion dollars, equal to the GDP of the 28 poorest countries. Its goal is to double every five to seven years. Given its present rates of ownership and control, how can this happen without leading to monopoly control?

Public relations

These corporations employ the services of the biggest and most influential PR companies, who rebrand them as committed to sustainability, native wisdom and green principles. They are prepared to hire poor farmers to demonstrate in favour of biotechnology and against critics like Vandana Shiva, as they did at the World Summit for Sustainable Development in Johannesburg in 2002. It turned out that the demonstration was organized by a right-wing London-based group linked to the Institute for Economic Affairs. Some of these PR companies specialize in email and web work, and are able to generate supposedly spontaneous critiques of articles in scientific journals

critical of GM or of biotechnology in general. Information promoting globalization and biotechnology is carefully managed.
Rupert Murdoch praises the way the think tanks which are so
often involved are all 'inspired with the principles of classical
liberalism that are fundamental to our civilisation'.

Directly related to corporate control are plummeting prices
for agricultural commodity markets. Producers, whether of
bananas or milk, coffee or pigs, are faced with immiserizing
growth; which means they must produce more but earn less.
Millions of farmers worldwide compete to supply fewer and
fewer huge buyers. All farmers are caught, and all, but especially those in the developing world, have the chagrin of seeing
huge profits made out of their products by western companies
through branding and re-exportation.

The role of supermarkets

Farmers are caught between the agribusiness corporations on
the one hand, and increasingly powerful supermarket chains
on the other. The top 30 grocers in the world control a third of
all food sales. WalMart, the world's largest retail company,
has sales bigger than all but 30 of the world's largest national
economies. In the US WalMart has driven 25 other supermarket chains to bankruptcy. Its power is so great that relatively
small players like Sainsbury's simply cannot compete in the
drive for lower prices. Ironically in Britain in 2005, it is complaining about the market share of Tesco, and objecting to
monopoly power!

The larger the player, the greater the discount they can
obtain. The impact on suppliers can be so serious that the
prime minister of St Vincent and Grenadines wrote to Tony
Blair and the UK Office of Fair Trading protesting against
Asda/WalMart's banana price war and the risk to his island's
economy if Asda took over Safeway. When Tesco cut its banana

prices by 30 per cent it passed this on to its importers. The effect is that plantation workers now receive well below the living wage. Supermarket chains are growing in power all over the world already controlling more than half of retail sales in Latin America, Thailand and Poland. Michael Hart, of the Small and Family Farms Alliance in Britain blames the low prices for farm goods on Tesco's near monopoly. As Friends of the Earth point out, the drive to lower prices impacts on farmers, farm workers, the environment and animal welfare.

Low prices, sanctimoniously proclaimed as being in the interests of the 'consumer' (a useful appeal for every shady practice), are only possible because risk is pushed back onto farmers and other suppliers. They include a whole range of unethical, if not illegal, practices such as delaying payment for produce, lowering prices at the last minute, buying less than the amount agreed to, threatening to remove farmers from supply lists, charging high-interest rates for credit, changing quality standards without adequate notice and even cancelling orders altogether. Fruit and vegetables are automatically scanned and and rejected even if only fractionally outside the required specification. Rejected fruit may go to juice at giveaway prices or simply be thrown away. Farmers are trapped because the supermarkets control so much of the retail market that they have few other outlets for their produce. Farmers speak of a 'master–servant' relationship with supermarkets and of a 'climate of fear'. This climate makes the code of conduct agreed to by supermarkets ineffective. Suppliers are frightened they will be delisted or that terms of trade will be worsened if they complain. Governments play along with the supermarket chains because cheap food keeps the voters happy. In fact, they not only play along, they invite them into government.

Although supermarkets sign up to supposed ethical codes of conduct, they actually market fair trade as consumer choice and do not adopt it as corporate standard. They also apply extra mark ups on fair-trade products on top of the extra they pay suppliers. The result of all this is that, as Isaiah put it, 'The spoil of the poor is in your houses' (3.14). Every 'consumer' is implicated.

Overseeing world trade

The organization responsible for overseeing world trade is the World Trade Organization (WTO), the last fruit of the attempt to produce a more just and more stable world order hammered out at Bretton Woods in 1944. That world was still one of competing nations, and indeed this still has some force, as when the US slapped tariffs on steel to protect its own industry from cheaper imports. The world in which the WTO finally emerged, however, was one in which corporations now exercised a new kind of power. Representatives from corporations staffed all of the groups which set out the US position, and more than 500 of them now attend every ministerial and have a much bigger voice than citizens' groups. The Codex Commission, which regulates food for the WTO, has 95 government delegates and 90 from the food industry. Meanwhile, 30 countries have no office at the WTO at all because they cannot afford one. When there are disputes three 'experts' adjudicate and, as was seen in the banana dispute between the EU and the huge American companies, the giant companies and the small producers were deemed to be 'like'. The whole procedure suggests the trial of Toad in *The Wind in the Willows*, with corporate experts as the weasels!

Rules framed by the WTO are aimed at preventing governments interfering with international trade. The chief brief of the organization is to further liberalization, to the benefit of corporations. 'Free' trade means the freedom of corporations to do what they will. The upshot is that every aspect of society is organized in a way which promotes the pursuit of corporate profit. WTO rules, for example, take precedence over social justice and environmental considerations. Corporations can sue countries and many have won tens of millions of dollars for 'unfair restraint of trade'. Thus laws in England and France restricting the use of asbestos were challenged by Canada, which exports it; laws in Europe restricting the import of timber from old-growth forests were challenged by Canada; European laws banning the import of genetically modified organisms were successfully challenged by the US; a Canadian ban on the petrol additive MMT, which can cause impairments to movement and speech, was overturned and Canada paid millions to the corporation making it; legislation protecting small shops in Japan was repealed on the threat of a WTO case instigated by the US.

With regard to agriculture it is the brief of the IMF, the WTO and the agribusiness corporations to persuade developing countries that self-sufficiency is not a practical answer to their problems. The British government (that is, taxpayers) is paying millions of pounds to a free trade organization, the Adam Smith Institute, to promote free trade in developing countries as the answer to their problems. These countries are caught from both directions. On the one hand they are often swamped with cheap imports. South Korea and the Philippines, for example, were forced to allow the import of cheaper US rice. Imports like this make survival for small farmers impossible and millions have left the land. Under free trade doctrine these peasants reskill, help earn more foreign exchange and allow for the import of food, but in fact, as a WCC study in 1999 found, food security consistently declines under trade liberalization. The lower cost of the imported food takes no account either of the social and environmental costs of production in, say, the

US, nor of the benefits of the local system. It thinks only in terms of monetary cost.

On the other hand exports are recommended, to improve trade balances and allow the import of high technology. Around the world, a million hectares a year are converted to cash crops. Millions of poor people have seen their food security decline because of this trade. Indian farmers are urged to grow flowers rather than food. But foreign exchange earnings for flowers pay for only a quarter of the amount of food which could be grown better at home. After ten years of bullish exports Indian farmers are worse off, more heavily indebted, have lower prices, and a correspondingly higher suicide rate. A Kenyan study found that trade liberalization benefited only the rich and not the poor. The switch to tobacco farming in Kenya has meant that food production has suffered and formerly self-sufficient areas now need famine relief. Diseases of malnutrition are once again prevalent. Relying on cash crops means that a country is subject to the vicissitudes of the market. The economies of whole countries have been brought to ruin because the price of coffee has fallen by 80 per cent (though not in our supermarkets). Overproduction was blamed but this was because Vietnam, at the behest of the World Bank, had become the world's second largest producer. Coffee is one of the key cash crops controlled by huge corporations. Bananas are another. Chiquita controls a quarter of the global banana market while Dole claims to be the largest producer. The economies of scale they are able to introduce, which follow from an insistence on non-unionized labour, make it impossible for smaller growers to obtain an economic price, which means in turn that they cannot pay a legal minimum wage. Brazil, Argentina and India all export food and have millions malnourished. In the North American Free Trade Association (NAFTA) Mexico sacrificed protection for the peasant farming sector, and for food security itself, in exchange for increased exports of fruit and vegetables.

An economic system predicated on trade dogma is profoundly irrational leading Britain, for example, to export and import roughly the same quantities of pork and butter, at huge environmental cost, and to set aside millions of acres and import food which could perfectly well be grown on that land. At the height of the English apple season more than half of supermarket apples are imported. The original justification of comparative advantage is nowhere in view. The system is in every respect lunacy.

The fallacy of free trade

The systematic distortions in the market owing to corporate power show that appeals to 'free trade' are specious. Free trade ideology harks back to Adam Smith's world of a multitude of small traders and of national capital. Today's reality is of a smaller and smaller number of increasingly powerful players and of global capital. Free trade is the slogan behind which the powerful exploit the weak. In fact, of course, everyone knows it is a fiction. The former US Trade Representative Mickey Kantor remarked: 'I don't believe in free trade. There is no such thing. We want rules based trading systems, not free trade. Free trade is chaotic. I don't know anybody that wants free trade'. The Australian development economist Graham Dunkley argues that the benefits of free trade are overrated and its costs underestimated, its main effects being undemocratic, 'non-consensual' social change. In the name of free trade the assets of the common treasury are being enclosed, privatized and used for the personal gain of a tiny minority.

The core of the free market gospel is greater prosperity all round, and there is no doubt that in some respects there have been real gains. On the other hand, social disparity is greater than ever. The top fifth of global population has 86 per cent of world GDP and 83 per cent of the world's wealth. The next fifth has 11 per cent of the world's wealth; the bottom three-fifths have only six per cent of the world's wealth between them. A quarter of the world's population manages on less than a dollar a day. In the US the financial wealth of the top one per cent now exceeds the combined household wealth of the bottom 95 per cent. The pay gap between top executives and their average employees in the largest US companies widened from 42 to 1 in 1980 to 531 to 1 in 2000. Herman Daly comments that when disparity reaches these kinds of levels the fabric of society starts to disintegrate. The number of Americans living in poverty has grown in each year of the Bush presidency and now stands at 36 million. In Britain, meanwhile, a report from the Office of National Statistics in December 2004 showed that the wealthiest one per cent of the population increased its share of the national wealth by three per cent between 1997 and 2002. On average, each individual in that one per cent was £737,000 better off than at the beginning of New Labour's reign. During the same period, the poorest 50 per cent's proportion of the national wealth shrank from seven per cent to five per cent.

Principalities and powers

Theologically we have to remember the warning of Ephesians that 'Our struggle is not against enemies of flesh and blood, but against the rulers, against the authorities, against the cosmic powers of this present darkness, against the spiritual forces of evil in the heavenly places' (Ephesians 6.12). Walter Wink has taught us that the language of 'the powers' describes the accumulated spiritual power, the 'personality', of nations, cultures, corporations or other powerful groupings. Today the principalities and powers are above all the structures of world trade, and in particular the spirituality, the worldview, behind them. They are, in Wink's terms, created, fallen and can be redeemed.

They are *created*: We need structures for trade. Complete self-sufficiency is neither possible nor desirable.

But they are *fallen*: The present structures of world trade damage both people and planet.

But, again, they can be *redeemed*. How?

Fair trade

One reads many appeals to the power of the consumer but consumer choice is an inadequate means of curbing corporate power and in any case, we should not accept the levelling discourse of the citizen as consumer. We are citizens with ethical dreams and responsibilities and visions of the human good which go beyond the market. Precisely for this reason the idea of fair trade has been catching on, an idea which, whether people realize it or not, goes back to medieval notions of the just wage and the just price. Fair trade means a guaranteed minimum reward for product and labour and relationships which can be relied upon. Paying growers a price which allows a decent standard of living is to deny the central market doctrine that the market will find its own level, no matter how low. According to market dogma weak or inefficient producers will be forced out and, with a smaller number of producers, a fair price will be realized again. But this fails to take account of distortions brought about by corporations and the WTO, and it pays no account of the huge social cost of unemployment or the environmental cost of industrial agriculture. It measures efficiency purely in financial terms.

The idea of 'fair' trade, by contrast, appeals to people's sense of fair play, and to the understanding that producers should get a reasonable return both for their labour and their product. It signals the normative reintroduction of ethics into economics, a return to the situation Adam Smith presupposed. It implies regulated markets, and it needs to be applied much more widely, to European agriculture, for example, as well as to developing world products. Proposals for regulated markets are in fact only proposals for *differently regulated* markets, for as it is the WTO regulates in favour of corporation interests. Graham Dunkley points out that managed trade characterized the two highest growth eras in human history, including the period from 1950 to 1975. Opposition to regulated trade is, in fact, not based on well-founded objections grounded in experience but on dogma. Regulated trade can help establish just prices, which is to say prices which cover the cost of production, remuneration of the farmer's labour and the multifunctional role of agriculture at one and the same time. The knock-on effect of agreeing to fair trade is to question unrestricted imports, because it is these which destabilize prices. Farmers' markets and community-supported agriculture are ways in which fair-trade policies are promoted but in truth it needs to become a model right across the economy.

Restoring democratic control

Fair trade cannot be established without the power of the corporations being tamed. At present they are overmighty subjects. Control needs to be wrested back from corporations towards democratic institutions which represent the whole population. Citizens' movements all over the world are increasingly asking this question and seeking to challenge corporate governance. Something can be done in terms of their legal accountability. As they are presently constituted they are primarily responsible to shareholders, but pressure groups are calling for legal changes which make them responsible for the social and environmental impacts of their policies. Corporate personhood needs to be abolished so that directors and managers can be held fully accountable for the actions of their companies. The political power of corporations also needs to be addressed by prohibiting the huge financial contributions corporations make to political parties and movements and by closing the revolving door between business and politics. Beyond this, given their enormous size and power, there is a strong case for UN monitoring of corporations, perhaps through an international court of economic justice. An international trade organization to ensure free and equal access to all forms of global trade and manage commodity stabilization schemes might be established more on the lines that Keynes proposed at Bretton Woods.

Trading creatures 'by nature'

Neo-liberal economics rests, I argued, on pseudo-theological redefinitions of what it means to be human, of ethics and of providence. We are all supposed to be 'by nature' trading creatures. Graham Dunkley argues, by contrast, for what he calls the 'Gandhian Propensity' for people to seek reasonable social justice, protection of cultural–spiritual traditions and maintenance of the community's natural environment. What is at issue are not 'iron laws of economics' (there is no such thing), but competing visions of the human. The rage of neo-liberals at any challenge to the market, the claim that one defies reality in even thinking outside the neo-liberal box, is an idolatrous rage. The proposals I have suggested represent small steps in the direction of an alternative to the hegemony of the free market. 'To envision and pursue radical alternatives to the monoculture market economy', writes Brewster Kneen, 'alternatives that will meet the requirements of ecological sustainability, human community, and Biblical faith, is not utopian. It is utopian, however, to think that we can solve the problems of the grow-ing destruction of Creation, increasing hunger and deprivation, and deepening concentration of wealth and power in the hands of a tiny fraction of the world's people, with more debt, more technology, more oppression, and yet more exhortation to be competitive and productive.'

It is still true, as it was in Aristotle's day, that economics is essentially about the housekeeping of what we have come to realize over the past half century is a global village. At the moment it is a caste-divided village, with a super-rich quarter, a middle-class area, and then the shanties for the rest. This dis-tortion of what economics is really about arises essentially from greed, which Aristotle diagnosed as a puerile disorder. What we have to bring about, as the WCC has demanded, is a trans-formation from this power-centred economy to a life-centred one, in which the relationships of the global village are ordered justly. In essence it is a question of the redemption of econo-mics, of the recovery of its true vocation and a move away from the protection of vested interests.

For further reflection and action

- Does the way trade is organized in our area reflect love of God and love of neighbour? If not, what might we do about it?

- Are there things we can do to support poor communities in the majority world, for example by fair trade, or by lobbying?

- Are there things we can do to make our own shopping prac-tices more just and equitable?

3

Daily bread

If one wanted a single phrase to sum up the message of the
Hebrew Bible it might be 'life and life in all its fullness' (John
10.10). YHWH is the God of life, the source of all life, according
to Genesis. That is the reason that all the words for 'sin' in the
Hebrew Bible also refer, in one way or another, to behaviour
which destroys or diminishes life. As the redeemer (the *go'el* of
Job 19.6) YHWH is the one who protects, defends and restores life.

God's concern for life is reflected in part by the provision of
food, the most common word for which, in the Hebrew Bible,
is *lechem*, bread, reflecting the Mediterranean staple. Wheat,
along with rice and maize, is one of the three crops which feed
the world, together giving us 'the staff of life'. The concern with
food is hardly surprising, for food is fundamental: no food, no
life. Genesis begins with the provision of food for humans,
whether in relation to the whole ecological system (Genesis 1)
or by envisioning them as placed in a garden which they have
to till and keep (Genesis 2) and ends with an extended story
about food security – the Joseph story. The key story of the
Hebrew Bible, the exodus, turns precisely on this. The exodus
stands between Abraham's journey to 'the Negev' on the one
hand, with its sense of wide open spaces for pastoral nomads
to graze their flocks, and the later conquest of Canaan on the
other, with the promise of a land flowing with milk and honey.
Famine, and the threat to survival, is the lynch pin of the whole

extended story. The issue of food security is dealt with by forward planning (Joseph's dreams), government intervention, and the building of store cities where surplus is accumulated to deal with lean years. The story is about providence: Joseph tells his brothers, 'God sent me before you to preserve life' (Genesis 45.5). But God 'provides' by inspiring Joseph to plan for the future. Divine intervention takes the form of human prudence. As the prologue to Israel's founding narrative, the story was a stark reminder that food could not be taken for granted and that careful provision was essential.

Food security

Food security is still a vivid memory for the older generation in Europe, and in England 'dig for victory' has passed into the collective memory. The date of the framing of the UN Declaration of Human Rights, 1948, meant that food security was one of the key aspects of the declaration. Later, the World Food Summit in 1996 defined this as meaning every person should have food that is available at all times, which is nutritionally adequate in terms of quality and variety and is acceptable within a given culture. In the same way, when the Common Agricultural Policy was first framed food security was one of the concerns. Postwar Europe was not interested in butter mountains and wine lakes but self-sufficiency. In Europe today, food security is thought to be a dead issue. According to Britain's Department of Food and Rural Affairs (DeFRA) food security is neither necessary nor desirable. For the minister in charge, Margaret Beckett, it is a matter of being able to pay for food – a classic definition of someone who thinks food comes from supermarkets and who is unaware of any relation to agriculture! In many parts of the world, and especially in Africa, however, food security is a very live issue. Even in Britain and the US many people go hungry and it is a well-known fact that among the poor the need to pay the rent, clothe the family and pay for transport to work takes precedence over food. In the US, the largest producer and exporter of food in the world, 11 million people are food insecure and hungry and a further 23 million are hovering close to the edge of hunger. For each of the past five years the world has consumed more grain than it has produced, by drawing on existing stocks. That situation is obviously unsustainable.

Food security is a global and not a national issue, and turns on the crucial question of the convergence of rising population on the one hand, with decreasing amounts of fertile land on the other. Currently population grows by 80 million per year. To feed 80 million people you need to expand the grain harvest by 21 million tons per year. There are two problems with this. The first is that the amount of fertile land is finite. Arable land constitutes one tenth of our world; meadows and pastures one quarter; forest and woodland one third; urban areas, deserts and ice caps the final third. But not only is the land available to produce food finite, *it is also shrinking*, in the face of desertification, overgrazing, salination and urbanization. Twenty-five million acres is lost each year due to all these factors. In the Great Plains of the US overtilling means that every acre is losing seven tons of topsoil every year. It cannot be simply replaced from the local garden centre. It is a precious commodity: it takes between 250 to 1,200 years to form an inch of soil. Desertification is driving three million people per year off their homes. Meanwhile, urbanization takes more and more good agricultural land. The Council for the Protection of Rural England estimates that a sixth of England's land area has already been lost to urban areas, and that we are currently losing 11,000 hectares per year. By mid-century a fifth of England could be urbanized.

Food security and the market

Where world population is going to plateau no one can be sure. The UN guess suggests nine and a half billion, though that may be conservative. If we are going to feed nine or ten billion we will have to rely on the world's fertile areas. It is true that food production has soared in the past 50 years, but not in 49 developing countries, where it failed to keep pace with population growth. The issue of food security is discussed in Europe in the context of a crisis of overproduction, which is the reason for policies such as set-aside. That crisis is, in relation to any projections of the growth of world population, a very temporary affair. Some time in the next 30 or 40 years we are going to have to address the question of feeding eight or ten billion in a world where fertile land is at a premium. The Food and Agriculture Organization (FAO) estimates that we need to double global output to keep track of rising numbers and present shortfalls. Meanwhile, as might be imagined, the world's economic leaders believe that the answer to all problems is to be found in the market. The president of Cargill Asia Pacific told a World Bank forum on China: 'China needs to choose whether it will adhere to past ideas of food self-sufficiency or if it will accelerate its integration into the global food system . . . A clear embrace of an open food system linked to world markets and based on its own agricultural comparative advantage would be a wise choice for China'. The answer to food security is to hand control over to the corporations, a view which DeFRA also adopts.

Such faith in the market (i.e. corporate control) is rejected by a number of organizations representing small farmers. In France the Confédération Paysanne calls for food sovereignty, an intelligent protectionism, and the abandoning of the supposed export vocation of agriculture in the EU. The Via

Campesina wants the concept of food sovereignty to be recognized in international law and condemns the integration of agriculture into WTO accords. It insists on 'The rights of peoples, communities and countries to define their own agricultural labour, fishing, food and land policies which are ecologically, socially and economically and culturally appropriate to their unique circumstances'. In its statement at the Seattle round of the WTO it argued that neo-liberal agricultural policies threatened 'the very coherence' of the societies of its members and, by targeting agriculture, was destroying cultural identity.

In terms of the discussion in the first chapter, food security is bound up with ecosystem justice. If we do not take care of all the connections, food security will certainly be threatened. A small illustration of this (and a personal one, since I write as a beekeeper) is the current threat to bee populations in Europe, not just from diseases but from exposure to pesticides, especially Fipronil in France. Bee populations are currently in decline, but if they failed altogether much agriculture would go with them, because pollination would go with it. Maintaining food security, then, is a matter of keeping the bigger picture, the question of proper husbandry, in view.

Besieged by hunger

One of the reasons that food security is no longer taken seriously is that people born in the West since 1960 enjoy a unique position within history. Of course there are many people within western societies who are poor, and who don't know where the next penny is coming from. At the same time in most western societies some kind of welfare net is in place, no matter how under strain, and most of us have had the experience of shopping at supermarkets, have seen the huge trolleys groaning with every kind of foodstuff, from every corner of the world, wheeled, with some difficulty, to the car boot. This is the supermarket society.

Go back just over a century, however, and you have a very different picture. One of the best loved books of English pastoral, Flora Thompson's *Larkrise to Candleford*, was written by someone who grew up in a peasant hamlet in North Oxfordshire in the 1880s. She calls that generation 'the besieged generation'. What besieged them was hunger. In that village, and in most of the villages of the country, only the rich knew what it was to be full. Agricultural labourers and their families, who formed more than 40 per cent of the population, never knew what it was to be full. Young men 'took the Queen's shilling' because there was a promise of a full stomach. In Flora Thompson's part of the world every family kept a pig, which was the universal talking point – because it meant food.

That generation was repeating the experience of every previous one. Peter Brown, in his wonderful history of early Christianity, notes that the rise of monasticism has to be understood against the background of constant famine. Because of the frequency and compelling nature of hunger, to deprive oneself deliberately of food was viewed as the ultimate test of self-discipline. Food, not sexuality, was the real problem and the sin of our primal parents was not sex but greed. It is argued that it is because of the frequency of famines that we are programmed by evolution to eat fast and hard. In England between 1500 and 1600 one in six harvests was a failure, a figure more or less typical of pre-twentieth-century history. It was a key factor leading to the French revolution. As we have already seen, hunger is still a fact of life for about one eighth of the world population.

In the West, however, the supermarket society knows nothing about hunger. In fact the problem is now obesity. Seventeen per cent of UK women and 21 per cent of men are obese, and

46 per cent of men are overweight. In the US, 61 per cent of men are overweight and 20 per cent obese. One quarter of under-25s are obese. Diseases of affluence such as Type 2 diabetes and coronary heart disease are on the increase. Food-related conditions such as anorexia and bulimia have reached epidemic proportions. Every town, meanwhile, has its exercise clinics, its keep fit classes, and everywhere joggers pound the streets trying to burn off unnecessary fat. This is the other side of the obesity story. The 1880s generation would have looked on with astonishment.

The stories of the wilderness wanderings in the book of Numbers constantly return to hunger and thirst, contrasting it with the well-fed slavery of Egypt. Jesus teaches his disciples to pray for '*ton arton ton epiousion*'. The last word is unattested anywhere else in Greek and has generated volumes of commentary from the second-century onwards. To the extent that one can talk of agreement it seems that the phrase refers back to the story of the manna, where God gives Israel its food for the coming day. The conventional translation, 'daily bread', is therefore reasonably accurate, and preserves the sense that food is God's gift, something to be thankful for. Prayer for daily bread, and thankfulness for food, makes absolute sense against a background of food insecurity. It makes much less sense in the supermarket society.

Thankfulness for food

Thankfulness for food is something that characterizes most peasant cultures, and was once part of daily life in Christian Europe. The fundamental thankfulness involved in eating is one of the most secure things we know about Jesus of Nazareth. The central ritual act of Christianity is now most commonly known as 'the eucharist', from the Greek verb *eucharisteo*, to give thanks. It stems from a key action at the last supper where Jesus, following conventional Jewish practice, broke bread and gave thanks. Crucially, in the story of the supper at Emmaus, the disciples did not recognize Jesus until he gave thanks. This reveals thanksgiving as an absolutely characteristic, identifying action on Jesus' part. Grounded as he was in the traditions of his people, Jesus was a thankful human being, someone who attached special significance to giving thanks for food, and who for that very reason taught his disciples to ask for their daily bread – the opposite of taking it for granted or abusing it.

If food security is the first issue in the Hebrew Bible, the next, and related to it, is the understanding of *food as gift*. To understand daily bread as gift is a crucial part of what it means to live under grace rather than, as Paul puts it, under law. To know food as gift is not only to be aware of the immense amount of labour, of justice and injustice, which lies behind everything we eat. It is also about our self-understanding.

The 'fast food nation' anatomized by Eric Schlosser, which applies to the UK as well as to the US, represents a culture which knows nothing of food as gift. Amazingly diverse cuisines represent millennia of experimentation which, through the alchemy of art, turn virtually anything that can provide nourishment and which is not positively toxic into delicious food. Fast food, on the other hand, subjects food to the routinized processes learned first in car factories, cuts costs so that food is produced dangerously and unhealthily, pays as low wages as possible, and is made simply to be stuffed down one's throat. In 1970 Americans spent six billion dollars on fast food. In 2001 they spent 110 billion dollars. On any given day one quarter of the population visits a fast food restaurant.

Fast food is 'food on the go' – processed in order to be stuffed down before doing something more important. Compare the

Indian pavement dweller who will spread out his piece of cloth, sit down, and eat his two rice cakes and lentil sauce slowly and with reverence. Sacraments are sign acts. Stuffing one's face as one walks or sits in one's car is a sign act of disrespect, a contemptuous gesture to the very notion that creation is something to be grateful for, to be honoured and appreciated. In traditional societies food has rituals: the sabbath meal, 'Sunday dinner', feasts such as Thanksgiving and Christmas. These latter survive, of course, but outside the context of an understanding of gift they can become simply boorish occasions of over-indulgence. In the fast food society convivial meals are replaced by constant snacking, chewing and swigging from cans or bottles.

In this context the Italian 'slow food' movement is something we need to learn from. This is not just about an increasingly affluent society dining out more but about the ancient desire to share and to gift oneself through food, as told paradigmatically in the story of the three angelic visitors in Genesis 18. Seeing them Abraham jumps up and begs them to take a meal with him. When they say they are in a hurry and can't stay he presses them. Such hospitality, the story says, is hugely rewarding, not so much in the return of a quid pro quo, but in the establishment of a culture of courtesy and generosity, where people have the time to talk and the pleasure of giving and receiving. Anyone who has travelled in the Mediterranean or in Asia will know that this is not about a dinner party culture but was traditionally part of peasant culture where people who had next to nothing would press food on their guests which they would never dream of eating themselves, as a privilege. Here a gift really could be given because the possibility of making a return was just out of the question. This is not to pretend, of course, that such societies did not have many problems. It is not to romanticize peasant cultures. It is, nevertheless, to insist that there is something priceless we have lost in the shift to industrialized eating, something we need to recover.

The theme of food as gift and self-gift, and of thanksgiving for food, is beautifully expounded in the film *Babette's Feast*, based on the novella by Isak Dinesen. The film is set in a remote rural settlement in mid-nineteenth-century Denmark, affected by Grundtvig's pietistic revival. Two sisters preside over the village, keeping the memory of their minister father alive, and doing works of charity. Babette arrives as a refugee from the Paris Commune and it at once appears that she is a marvellous cook. After 14 years in the village, which is riven with jealousies, resentments and factions, Babette wins the Paris lottery. She asks the sisters' permission to provide them with a special meal, and they agree it is to be on the anniversary of their father's death, when they traditionally give a meal for the poor. She disappears for a few days, and the recipients of the sisters' charity at once notice the decline in diet. She returns with a huge cache of provisions, including a live turtle, a crate of live quails, and all sorts of wine. The sisters are horrified, as it contradicts their puritan ethos. They gather their small community around them and they unite against this threat. They agree to eat as if they are not eating, and never to speak of the meal. In the course of the tale it transpires that Babette was formerly the famous cook at the L'Anglais restaurant in Paris. Though the old people do not appreciate the fine details, the meal overcomes their puritan scruples, restores their bonhomie, and brings them together again.

One of the themes of the film is the idea of gift, and the insistence that gifts cannot be given except through matter, and in particular food. Babette gives herself through the meal. The preparation of the meal functions as a parable for living: the dead creatures are cut up, lovingly prepared and artfully served. There is only life through death, but it is death in the service of love. Not so much the meal, but the preparation of the meal is sacramental. The comparison of life to food is a theme which goes right back to Ignatius of Antioch, comparing himself to the grain about to be crushed for the sake of Christ. Augustine also uses it.

As well as food as gift, Israel also celebrated *good food*, as in this account of the well-watered Jordan valley:

> The Lord your God is bringing you into a good land, a land with flowing streams, with springs and underground waters welling up in valleys and hills, a land of wheat and barley, of vines and fig trees and pomegranates, a land of olive trees and honey, a land where you may eat bread without scarcity, where you will lack nothing . . . You shall eat your fill and bless the Lord your God for the good land that he has given you.
> (Deuteronomy 8.6–10)

In the New Testament Paul appeals to the fertility of creation as one of the evidences for God's existence. He tells the crowd in Lystra: 'God has not left himself without a witness in doing good – giving you rains from heaven and fruitful seasons, and filling you with food and your heart with joy' (Acts 14.17).

Gluttony and justice

There is nothing wrong with plenty as such – quite the contrary. The Bible, too, has much to say about the house of feasting, and when the Son of Man, or Human One came he was known by his critics as 'a glutton and a drunkard'. Good food is food which is not just nourishing but delicious and artfully prepared. Such food is part of the fullness of life. There is no doubt that such a statement runs counter to an important strand of Christian thinking. Over the centuries an ascetic ethic developed which was deeply suspicious not only of sexuality but of the pleasures of the table. John Wesley epitomizes this in his advice that, given the choice of two dishes, 'by the rule of self-denial, you ought to eat of that which you like the least'. To an extent this was about asceticism for its own sake but it was also related to a concern for justice. The reason gluttony was considered one of the seven deadly sins was not because overindulgence was frowned on, but because behind gluttony stood avarice and dominance. To resist gluttony was to seek more just and more truly human relations. Suspicion of the pleasures of the table was well-founded because they were often only available to the rich.

When a contemporary food writer tells us that we should 'get back to the sheer joy of eating . . . license ourselves to be as selfish and as greedy as possible in obtaining maximum flavour from our food and maximum pleasure from our cooking and eating' and when we read about the body as 'a conduit and source of hedonistic pleasure and release and narcissistic display' those old suspicions are once again reawakened. But we can recall Karl Barth, eating in Paris after World War II, describing the meal as 'a devastating refutation of materialism'. If we understand the incarnation properly, God taking flesh, this carries with it, as the Church has insisted from Irenaeus onwards, an affirmation of the material. We must distinguish between being 'materialistic' – which means making goods, things, our god – and reverencing the world of bodies and matter which the Lord God has given us. Such reverence was what the iconoclast controversy in the eighth century turned on.

In relation to food, John Wesley and Francis of Assisi notwithstanding, I would say that the need to be gourmets follows from the incarnation! As food writers like Elizabeth David have demonstrated, good food does not have to be expensive food. In fact, much of today's haute cuisine emerges from peasant cooking. The association of peasant farmers, the Via Campesina, speaks of eating and producing quality products for its own people as 'a political act'. We could add that it was a faith act. We need a word other than 'gourmet' to express the proper appreciation of good food which is not luxury and self-indulgence but a proper respect for God's gifts.

The idea that cooking is truly a work of art, more akin to music than to painting, in that it has to be recreated afresh at each performance, but working from the same 'score' (i.e. a recipe) is another theme of *Babette's Feast*. Art is transcendence. In music bits of wood, bone, catgut, etc. 'speak' sublimely. In cooking, as the film emphasizes, your stomach can be filled, by average cooks like the sisters, but there can also be a transcendent dimension in which gluttony is left behind. The physical *becomes* the spiritual, an idea applied by the film to the meal, again a theme close to incarnation.

In the UK we now spend only 15 minutes a day preparing food as opposed to three hours in the 1930s. We eat fewer vegetables than any other European country and most of our favourite foods are processed. In 2000 £596 million was spent on advertising food in the UK, of which £4.4 million was spent on fresh fruit and vegetables, while £131m (28 per cent) went on advertising cereals, cakes, biscuits, potato crisps and snacks. More than 80 per cent of bread is produced by two firms and only 3,500 craft bakers remain, compared with ten times that number in France. The present campaign to introduce fresher, more nutritious and more local food into schools is in this respect encouraging.

Should we be vegetarians?

Is good food vegetarian food? Religious traditions such as Hindu Saivism have thought so but neither Judaism nor Christianity have agreed. The Priestly narrators clearly believed that creation was originally vegetarian. In God's blessing of man and woman God says: 'See, I have given you every plant yielding seed that is upon the face of all the earth, and every tree with seed in its fruit; you shall have them for food'. The animals likewise are given 'every green plant for food' (Genesis 1.29–30). After the flood this is modified:

> The fear and dread of you shall rest on every animal of the earth, and on every bird of the air, on everything that creeps on the ground, and on all the fish of the sea; into your hand they are delivered. Every moving thing that lives shall be food for you; and just as I gave you the green plants, I give you everything. Only, you shall not eat flesh with its life, that is, its blood.
>
> (Genesis 9.2–4)

In this narrative we have the sense that killing is never normal, never to be taken for granted. Flesh-eating is regarded as a permission, not a right, and kosher killing is a sign or sacrament of this. Isaiah famously dreamed of an end to all violence, and a return to the original paradisal state, where no creature preys on another (Isaiah 11.6–9). The permission to kill is one of the many aspects of food as gift, for a gift cannot be taken for granted.

Were the Priestly writers around today, would they be vegetarian, on the grounds that humans can live by vegetables and staples alone, and needless killing should be avoided? I think on the whole they probably would not. There are two reasons for keeping meat as part of the food chain. In the first place, if we eliminated the animals, apart from those in game reserves, this would mean a colossal change to the world's ecology. What is not grazed would have either to be mowed or left to go wild. Further, much of the world which currently supports life could no longer do so, for it cannot support crops – England's Lake District is a case in point. Second, and relatedly, as Colin Tudge argues, in fields and hedgerows we have colossal quantities of energy which we cannot harvest because we cannot eat it.

Ruminants process this for us, converting cellulose into food we can eat. I suspect the Genesis writers would feel the force of these arguments, but they would insist on permission, on the sanctity of all life, and not just human life, on food as gift.

This would mean, for example, that they would be appalled by factory farming, the conveyor belts on which thousands of chickens a day are hung upside down on the way to the electrocution bath, the huge abattoirs in which animals scent blood and death. If we thought about it we would know that these processes imply a disrespect for life; they are part of a culture which, in the interests of profit and cheap food, reduces animals simply to matter. Traditionally farmers never treated animals in this way. Animals were reared for food and duly killed but with a proper sense of their dignity and the fact that we live by their gift. 'The slaying of animals', said Karl Barth, 'is really possible only as an appeal to God's reconciling grace, as its representation and proclamation . . . the killing of animals in obedience is possible only as a deeply reverential act of re-pentance, gratitude and praise on the part of the forgiven sinner in face of the One who is Creator and Lord of man and beast. The killing of animals, when performed with the permission of God and by his command, is a priestly act of eschatological character'. The sense of reverence for life which Barth expresses has been lost in the world of plastic-wrapped food, where any connection with the animal from which the meat came is erased as far as possible.

Healthy eating

Good food is also *healthy food*, something which may well have been one of the concerns behind the list of prohibited foods in Leviticus. There are a number of things at issue here, widely canvassed in the western media. I have already noted the concern with obesity in the US and UK. This is partly to do with eating the wrong kind of food but it is also to do with eating too much relative to the amount of physical work, or exercise, we are taking. For most of us our needs are around 2,500 calories a day. If we eat more than that the body deals with it by turning it into fat. The only way to keep weight within bounds is to match daily intake with daily needs. The Bible shares with many ancient cultures a counsel of moderation: 'Let your moderation be known to all', Paul tells the Christians in Philippi (Philippians 4.5). To espouse the virtue of moderation is not to be opposed to the enjoyment of food. Indeed André Simon, a French gastronome of the 1930s, wrote: 'Gastronomy stands or falls by moderation. No gourmand and no glutton can be a gastronome'.

The relation between poverty and obesity, however, shows clearly that much of the food we eat is in itself unhealthy. If we eat fast food and ready-prepared food then the chances are we are eating food full of saturated and processed fats, highly refined carbohydrates and sugars which load us with calories without providing nutrients. High fructose syrup plays a part in much of what we eat and drink and ready meals consist of 15 per cent sugars. The best advice seems to be to eat as widely varied a diet as possible and to eat everything in moderation. This was something that Church rules on fasting historically promoted. In medieval Europe there were 150 fast days a year, which forced people to eat fish, or vegetables and pulses.

Quite apart from food which is unhealthy because it is full of fructose syrup, we need food that is free of additives and antibiotics. In 2002 a report found that food molecules act like hormones, and can cause mental imbalances ranging from attention-deficit and hyperactivity disorder to serious mental illness. Links between junk food and hyperactivity are well-established. By contrast, providing children with organic food at school has been found to lead to better behaviour.

The routine use of pesticides in farming means that poison residues are also common in food and may be related to the soaring depression rates in western cultures. In Britain the use of pesticides has increased by 30 per cent in the past ten years. Equally, in today's industrialized agriculture, livestock are routinely fed antibiotics to make them grow faster, produce more milk, and to enable them to be kept in conditions which are inappropriate. Roughly half the 25,000 tons of antibiotics produced in the US are used in raising animals for human consumption. The US Centre for Disease Control says antimicrobial resistance is a serious clinical and public health problem there. In the UK the House of Lords notes that there is a continuing threat to human health from the imprudent use of antibiotics in animals. Recurring food scares, especially those connected with *E. coli*, are, as Eric Schlosser argues, bound up with mass production and a fast food industry driven by antipathy to anything which might cut profits.

Food and culture

As well as being good, and healthy, food should be *culturally rich*. French farmers have insisted, in the dispute over whether Europe would be forced by the WTO to accept hormone-fed beef, that food is not a mere commodity. Giles Luneau comments, 'in eating, humans inscribe themselves in the cycles of the universe, and this is far more profound and basic than just making money. Wheat was growing long before coins were cast'. Cultural richness is threatened by the lunacy of the market. In the UK two-thirds of apple orchards have been lost in less than 30 years. There are over 6,000 varieties of apple, but only ten are in the supermarkets and 70 per cent of the apples are Cox and Bramley. *The Ecologist* quotes a US spokesman at the WTO as saying that trade liberalization will not stop until 'foreigners' (sic) start to think, act and shop like Americans. If one extends that to food one could hardly imagine a more dismal and unappetizing fate. Brewster Kneen, by contrast, talks of a 'proximity principle', that food should be consumed as close to the point and condition of production as possible: 'Maximum nutritional quality, maximum food security, maximum energy efficiency, and maximum return to those who contribute most to the food production process can be achieved in this way'.

Luneau's point is instantiated by the festivals we read of in the Hebrew Bible, and by Jesus' use of the Passover meal at the critical moment with his disciples. We remind ourselves of this every time we celebrate the eucharist. At the same time an experience of the South African theologian John de Gruchy puts the question of culturally rich food in an interesting light. A Capetown law firm decided to run a series where a member of a different faith community would come and talk about their tradition, and an appropriate meal would be served. For the Jews and the Hindus this was no problem; the Muslims served halal meat and middle-eastern food. But what was Christian food? The firm ended up serving roast beef, which would have puzzled St Paul! An endorsement of cultural richness, however, comes from Pentecost. The point of the story in Acts 2 is not that everyone could understand what was being said because everyone had access to a new form of Esperanto, a sort of McDonaldization of culture, but on the contrary, that everyone heard the gospel message in their own tongue. Different cultures, and therefore different cuisines, were endorsed at Pentecost, a point that the eighteenth-century German thinker Herder seized on in insisting that the variety of cultures was a gift of the Holy Spirit.

Against the grain of the Christian tradition I have argued that a proper appreciation of the material means that Christians ought to be gourmets. There is, however, an important qualification.

Bonhoeffer insisted that we could not sing plainchant if we did not cry out for the Jews. In the same way, we cannot be free to take food seriously unless we remember that a quarter of the world population is living on less than a dollar a day, and that 30,000 children are dying each day from hunger and preventable diseases. Food, in other words, has to be *just*. It is this fact, I suspect, which makes many Christians resile from taking food too seriously. The point that the gift of plenty is contingent on practices of justice is made frequently in scripture: '*If you follow my statutes and keep my commandments*' there will be plenty for all, say the authors of Leviticus (Leviticus 26.3). Jesus' depiction of God as the giver: 'pressed down, overflowing', draws on the description of Leviticus, where the harvesters can barely keep pace with the abundance of the crop. It is a key part of the realization of shalom, that situation of peace and justice which is God's will for Israel (Leviticus 26.6).

Jesus' insistence that 'Man shall not live by bread alone, but by every word that proceeds from the mouth of God' (Matthew 4.4) or his command in John to work not for the food which perishes but for the food that endures for eternal life (John 6.27) is not opposed to this. The word that proceeds from the mouth of God is, of course, the whole Hebrew Bible, the heart of which is the promise of shalom, peace with justice. To eat justly is to share one's bread with the hungry (Isaiah 58.7). By the same token to give food or drink to the poor, is to give it to Christ (Matthew 25.37). The food that endures to eternal life, therefore, is behaviour which honours God the Creator. What Jesus (or John) has in mind is the fact that over and over again greater wealth has been shown not to correlate with greater happiness. What makes for life is just relationships and societies, the pattern of satisfying work which comes out of that. The food that endures for eternal life is thus directly related to food for my neighbour.

Waste

Just food is food which is not wasted. The supermarket society, however, is a profoundly wasteful society. According to a report in July 2005 Britain's farmers are being forced to throw away as much as one third of their fruit and vegetables because they do not conform to supermarket standards. The director of the Soil Association said: 'The supermarkets want food that looks like it never came out of the ground. Much of it is purely cosmetic – farmers are being driven out of business simply because of natural skin blemishes or slightly odd shapes'. The Somerfield chain sets out its criteria for cauliflowers over three pages, including a demand that all should be 12 to 16 centimetres and uniform in colour with only two spots per leaf. Tesco tested potatoes with a 'brightness meter' to see if their skin was shiny enough! Much of Britain's home-grown fruit and vegetables end up in landfill. Of the five million tons of food grown for the supermarkets one fifth is lost in packing, grading and processing. Milk which is over quota is poured down the drain; fish which is over quota thrown back in the sea; food which is past its sell by date in the supermarkets is thrown out – health and safety regulations mean that it can no longer be given to pigs, the traditional way of recycling food. Ten millennia of knowledge about the need not to waste and the preciousness of food are dispensed with at the very same time that people die of hunger.

The continuing poverty of a quarter of the world population is related to the justice issue. It is related to the fact that the global economy treats food like any other commodity, which for the sake of economic efficiency must be sold wherever the highest price can be obtained. This means poor people go hungry while surrounded by fertile land that produces luxury crops for the rich. Today 61 per cent of Indian children under five are malnourished but India is a major food exporter. In his seminal work on famines Amartya Sen showed how, in the modern world at least, famine was essentially about distribution. India exported grain during its greatest famine, as did Ireland in the great famine. In both cases hundreds of thousands of human lives were sacrificed to the market. The eucharist contradicts this market logic. It is a sign act in which everyone gets an equal share. It is a sacrament of Israel's vision of how the earth ought to be divided and used equally for the good of all God's people.

Just food is food which is targeted at the common good, at the recognition of the crucial role food plays in human life. It is not food which is produced primarily for profit. Today, as a result of the privatization of the past three decades, publicly funded research on food has fallen and private research has increased. Large food businesses keep their results private in order to make a profit from them. The National Food Alliance measured attendance at Codex Alimentarius meetings and found that more corporations were represented than countries. Of more than 2,500 participants in Codex meetings 660 represented industry interests and 26 public interest groups.

Just food is food which repays the grower. We currently spend less on food than we did 20 years ago. Where, in the mid-twentieth century, it took 35 per cent of income, it now takes ten per cent. This seems good for the central figure of modern culture, the consumer, but the price that is paid is the ruin and even the death of the grower – the reason that farmers are more likely to commit suicide than other professions is that they can no longer make a living. Politicians zealously guard cheap food because it promotes a feel-good factor, but food which is sold for less than the cost of production is unjust food. To take food justice seriously will mean that we have to be prepared to pay more for it.

Just food is also food which respects ecosystem justice. This is, above all, the question of food miles. A DeFRA report in July

2005 found that food miles in Britain have risen by 15 per cent in the decade to 2002. In Britain people now drive nearly 900 miles per annum to shop. Supermarket lorries travel a billion miles a year. Between 1978 and 2000 the distance travelled by lorries doubled. Air freight is the fastest growing sector, a traffic encouraged by the zero rate of tax on aircraft fuel. Carbon dioxide emissions are six times higher for air transport than they are for road and rail. Absurdities abound, like the fact we import and export roughly the same quantities of butter and bacon. The British Potato Council estimates that the UK imports about 350,000 tonnes of potatoes a year, many coming when British potatoes are in season. This pushes British growers out of business. The 'logic' of this is the need for export markets and foreign exchange, but in terms of ecojustice and intergenerational equity it makes no kind of sense at all. In an attempt to prop up market prices apple orchards have been grubbed up all over England, with grants from the EU, so that (less tasty) apples can be imported. All kinds of food which can be better produced here is in fact imported. Ninety-five per cent of all fruit and half of all vegetables eaten in the UK come from abroad. As Professor of Food Policy, Tim Lang, puts it, 'Our so-called efficient food supply system is grossly wasteful. If the government doesn't take action to tackle this, all its proposals on climate change will be so much nonsense'. Foods that have been industrially produced and transported great distances seem cheaper because they never include their environmental costs. Supermarkets gain market share by selling cheap food, but cheap food is simply food where the costs to the environment, to producers and to human health are not factored in. If we added the costs in taxes for dealing with these problems we would find that food was not cheap at all.

'We pray for the coming of the kingdom, as Christ taught us'. This rubric precedes the saying of the Lord's prayer at every eucharist, one petition of which is our prayer for daily bread. The 'kingdom' is Jesus' way of talking the shalom language of the Hebrew Bible, the situation where God's will prevails in the warp and weft of ordinary life. The fact that the eucharist is the central act of Christian worship follows in part from the fact that table fellowship was a central part of Jesus' life and ministry. Concern with food, then, is as central to our liturgy as it is to our daily life. Indeed, it is central to the former in order that the centrality in the latter may be rightly ordered. I have tried to spell that out in terms of food security, and of an understanding of food as gift, and in terms of good food, healthy food, culturally rich food and just food. I turn next to what is always associated with food, in the Bible as elsewhere, namely water.

For further reflection and action

- Is our harvest supper based on local food and the finest cuisine?
- Are there members of the local community who could be helped to eat better?
- Are local schools signed up to local food?
- Given the global market in food what does it mean to 'eat the bread of justice'?
- If the Church is called to be a 'counterculture,' what does that mean for our food practices?

4

The water of life

———•◦•———

The Bible comes from an area where fertile valleys stand between
deserts, and the threat of drought is common. Hardly surpris-
ingly water, both as metaphor and reality, is a major theme,
though the sacrament which focuses on water, baptism, is more
concerned with cleansing than with water's necessity for survival. That theme is not absent, however. Both creation stories
reflect the centrality of water to life, and for the Priestly source
water is both threat and promise, indispensable but threatening
to overwhelm human life in devastating chaotic floods, a sense
with which many contemporaries can only too well empathize.
In the stories of the wilderness wanderings Israel is threatened
by death from lack of water and is saved by 'water from the
rock', a metaphor for Christ in the New Testament. The land to
which they come flows not just with milk and honey but with
streams, the basis of its fertility. On the way they need to buy
water from the Edomites and other inhabitants of Palestine.
Like many ancient peoples Israel knew the need to pay for water
to survive. Their dream, therefore, was of a world where all this
would lie beyond the market economy:

> Ho, everyone who thirsts,
> Come to the waters;
> And you that have no money!
> Come, buy wine and milk
> Without money and without price.
>   (Isaiah 55.1)

75

This promise is taken up in Revelation: 'To the thirsty I will give water without price from the fountain of the water of life' (Revelation 21.6).

For the prophets fresh water is a key metaphor for the new age. There will be rivers in the desert and water will flow from Jerusalem. God is understood as the one who gifts the water which makes farming possible:

> You visit the earth and water it,
> You greatly enrich it;
> The river of God is full of water;
> You provide the people with grain,
> For so you have prepared it.
> You water its furrows abundantly,
> Settling its ridges,
> Softening it with showers,
> And blessing it with growth.
>   (Psalm 65.9–10)

The rich use of water imagery in the Hebrew Bible is taken up by John in his account of Jesus' dialogue with the Samaritan woman: 'Everyone who drinks of this water will be thirsty again, but those who drink of the water that I will give them will never be thirsty. The water that I will give them will become in them a spring of water gushing up to eternal life' (John 4.13–14). By some this has been read in a gnostic sense, as denigrating the importance of ordinary water but, as in the words about the bread of life, it is more likely that it should be read in terms of the effect of living by the Word of God. As we saw in the previous chapter, what this means is the realization of shalom, peace and justice.

After the climate, water is the primary instance of the global commons which is either threatened by privatization or, in the perspective of Garret Hardin, can only be preserved by it. It is even more fundamental than food, for without it there is no food, and while we can survive for some time without food, we cannot survive without water. As the ancient epics recognized in various ways, water is the basis of life. It has no substitute.

There is, of course, plenty of water, but almost all of it – 97 per cent! – is in the oceans, and is saline. Some water is to be found in glaciers and icebergs; some is groundwater; less than one per cent, worldwide, is found in lakes and rivers. The weather system moves water round the planet through the constant cycle of evaporation and precipitation, in all transferring 40,000 cubic kilometres from the sea to the land each year. Water also plays a key role in keeping the planet cool, storing solar energy in the oceans, and reflecting back solar radiation through the frozen water at the poles.

Water stress

Water is not evenly spread around the world. Sixty per cent of fresh water is found in just nine countries. Water-sufficient countries are those which have more than 1,700 cubic metres per person. Between 1,000 and 1,700 cubic metres there is water stress and below 1,000 cubic metres there is water scarcity. It is estimated that within 20 years almost half the world's population will experience water scarcity. More and more countries get their water from groundwater, not surface water. About one third of water in France, Canada and the UK is supplied by aquifer. In countries like Saudi Arabia and Libya, and in parts of the US, the rate is much higher. In India, water is being pumped at twice the level it is replenished by rainfall. As noted in the first chapter, the weather system is already affected by the activities which cause global warming, especially the destruction of forests and urbanization.

Each of the world's six and a half billion people needs about five litres of water a day for drinking and cooking and another

25 to 45 litres a day for hygiene and health. Global consumption of water is doubling every 20 years, more than twice the rate of human population growth. Domestic use, however, accounts for only ten per cent of water use. The biggest user is agriculture, accounting for about 65 per cent of world water use. Most of this is used for irrigation on which 40 per cent of world food supply now depends. Industry claims the rest. A ton of steel uses 280 tons of water. It takes 400,000 litres of water to make one car. We only have to remember how global car use is expanding to see the impact that has. The hi-tech industry, which gives us our computers and their software, also uses a huge amount of water. Since water is a finite resource there is competition between agriculture and industry for supply. One ton of wheat requires 1,000 tons of water. If you measure the price of wheat against the price, say of computers, computers are far more cost-effective. China has made just this calculation and there has been an increasing shift of water use in China from agriculture to industry to power China's 'economic miracle'. It generates huge foreign exchange earnings but the question is how China's population is to be fed. Lester Brown, of the World Watch Institute, regards this as a threat to world food security.

A water class system

Although human needs are equal, rates of usage are not. In water use there is effectively a global class system. Where more than half the world's population gets by on about 50 litres a day, the average American uses 350 litres per day, and an Australian 570 litres per day. Californians have 560,000 swimming pools. Where millions of people still have to walk to collect water, much water is used to wash cars or keep golf courses green. On Palestine's West Bank, Israeli settlers have sprinklers to keep their lawns green while Palestinian women queue at taps. Israel has kept its parks green and grown cotton by limiting supplies to Palestinians in the Occupied Territories. Israeli per capita consumption is three times that of Palestinians. More than half of South Africa's raw water is used for white-dominated commercial agriculture, and half of that water is wasted in poor irrigation practices. About 12 per cent of South Africa's water is for domestic consumption, but of that amount more than half goes into white households, including water for gardens and swimming pools. Sixteen million South African women still have to walk at least one kilometre to get water. Water privatization in Puerto Rico has meant that poorer communities have gone without water while US bases and tourist resorts have an unlimited supply.

Polluting the springs

Much water is too contaminated for use. Eighty per cent of disease in poor countries is spread by consuming unsafe water. Ninety per cent of the developing world's waste water is discharged into untreated local rivers and streams; waterborne pathogens and pollution kill 25 million people every year. Malaria, cholera and typhoid are recurring more frequently. Indian rivers like the Ganges and the Brahmaputra are filled with bacteria and human sewage. About two million tons of waste are dumped every day into rivers, lakes and streams, and the total amount of waste water is more than that contained in the world's ten largest river basins at any given moment. More people means more pollution and it has been estimated that, if the problem is not addressed, almost nine times the amount of water used in irrigation will be lost to pollution by 2050.

Pollution is not just a problem for developing countries. Overuse of agricultural pesticides means that about 40 per cent of US rivers and streams are too dangerous for fishing, swimming or drinking. The US Environmental Protection Agency estimates that more than half the wells in the country are contaminated with pesticides. Nearly one fifth of the US population drinks tap water contaminated with lead, bacteria or other serious pollutants. In the free trade zone between the US and Mexico, factories dump toxic waste directly into rivers and streams. Clean water is so scarce babies and children drink Coke and Pepsi instead – a bizarre comment on the fact that there is no substitute for water! Three-quarters of Poland's rivers are so contaminated by chemicals, sewage and agricultural run-off that their water is unfit even for industrial use. All this helps to explain why the trade in bottled water is now worth 22 billion dollars annually. It is one of the fastest growing and least regulated industries in the world.

Scarcity

Water scarcity is increasing all over the world. Thirty-one countries, accounting for one third of the world's people, are now water-stressed. Over one billion have no access to clean drinking water and almost three billion have no access to sanitation. Some of the world's greatest rivers, including the Yellow River, the Rio Grande and the Colorado, now lose so much water upstream for irrigation that they fail to reach the sea. The Aral Sea, in Russia, and the Oasis of Azraq, in Jordan, which used to feed Amman, have dried up. Israel gets most of its water from the Sea of Galilee, but the lake is beginning to show saline infiltration because of overuse. Groundwater in the West Bank is also running out. Even water-rich England's major waterways are losing volume as a result of overuse of water and some are now less than a third of their average depth. About half the world's wetlands have also been lost over the last century.

The water of life

As water gets more scarce, the possibility of moving water around the world in vast tankers has been mooted, from water-rich to water-stressed countries. Alaska is the first jurisdiction to allow the commercial export of water. Quite apart from the 'water miles' involved, this may not be without environmental cost in terms of the disruption of breeding grounds and in any case it could not provide enough water for agricultural use. Some countries are looking to desalination but that is very expensive, fuel intensive and leaves concentrated salt deposit which then has to be disposed of.

Growing demand for food is the major reason for pressure on water resources. In a crop producing 20 tons fresh weight, 2,000 tons of water will pass though the roots. More people need more food and the Green Revolution saw a doubling in the area of irrigated land. Not all agricultural use is reasonable, however. Saudi Arabia's use of aquifer resources to turn itself into a grain exporting country, for example, is unsustainable. Here the theory of comparative advantage might come into its own and economists point out that purchasing grain is purchasing 'virtual water'. The question, of course, is what happens with countries that lack the wealth to import such virtual water.

Other uses of water are even less justifiable. In Texas aquifer resources were used to grow grain to feed cattle. Irreplaceable resources were thus being used to sustain intrinsically unhealthy diets. The Aral Sea, once the world's fourth largest lake, dried up because its water was used for irrigation for cotton, and whether that was a good exchange is very much a moot point. All around the world inefficient agriculture is responsible for much water loss. Lake Chad, in Africa, has shrunk by more than 90 per cent since 1960 due to irrigation. Poor irrigation practices, or irrigation in arid areas, damages the soil and creates dust bowls, or leads to build-ups of salt, which then make land unfit for farming. Every year it forces farmers to abandon two and a half million acres of farmland. Sandra Postel estimates that about ten per cent of the global grain harvest is being produced by using water supplies that are not being replenished. All over the world, but especially in the world's most populous countries, like India and China, countries are running huge water deficits – in India at the rate of 104 billion cubic metres a year. The growth rates such deficits make possible are, quite literally, built on sand.

Cities

The growth of mega-cities also poses a huge problem in terms of water resources. Madras (Chennai) in South India is a good example. Victorian engineers constructed reservoirs around the city for a projected population of 100,000. There are now eight million people. Mexico City now has 22 million people and depends on aquifers for 70 per cent of its water and is extracting water at 50 to 80 per cent faster than its rate of repletion. The world's cities grow at a rate of approximately 150,000 per day but, in terms of their most basic resource, they are simply unsustainable.

Dam-building has been one of the major ways of dealing with water in the twentieth century, especially for the production of hydro-electricity. New materials have meant a qualitative leap in their construction. In the last century 800,000 small dams were built and 40,000 large dams, more than 100 of them over 500 feet tall. Not only have they displaced many indigenous peoples, but they create the habitat for the parasites that cause schistomiasis and other water-borne diseases. As with the Nile, they often affect irrigation downstream. In the 1960s India built a dam at Farakka, diverting a portion of the Ganges from Bangladesh to flush silt from Calcutta's seaport, some 100 miles to the south. In Bangladesh, the reduced flow depleted surface water and groundwater, impeded navigation, increased salinity, degraded fisheries, and endangered water supplies and public health. The then Bangladeshi prime minister called it 'a gross violation of human rights and justice'. A treaty at the end of 1996 has since eased tensions between the countries and seen that Bangladesh is provided with more water. Critics of the World Bank's dam-building programme point out that it has made millions for the corporations, equipment suppliers and technical consultants of the construction and hydro-power industries for what are rather short-term gains, given the rates of siltation.

Water wars have been widely mooted for a couple of decades now, but Sandra Postel points out that they go back to the very beginnings of urban civilization: a water treaty is recorded between two Mesopotamian city states in 3100 BC. Rising populations have, however, brought a new urgency to the issue of water sharing. Some claim that the Arab–Israeli wars, and the continued occupation of the West Bank, are in fact about who controls the headwaters of the Jordan. Certainly, there cannot be peace in the Middle East until the issue of water is resolved. Downstream neighbours are complaining about upstream neighbours in Iraq, Syria, Pakistan and Egypt. G. W. Bush said before the Genoa G8 Summit in 2001 that he saw Canada's water like its energy reserves, to be shared with the US by pipeline. Not just countries, but also states within a country get into conflict over water, as in the ongoing argument between Karnataka and Tamil Nadu over the Cauvery in Southern India. As we have seen there is also conflict between industry and agriculture, town and country, between classes and racial groups, and between corporations and citizens. As the absolutely indispensable resource, the potential for conflict over water is huge.

Enclosure

In *The Wealth of Nations* Adam Smith observed that 'Nothing is more useful than water: but it will purchase scarce anything; scarce anything can be had in exchange for it'. Well, that was then. *Fortune* magazine noted in May 2000: 'Water promises to be to the 21st century what oil was to the 20th century: the precious commodity that determines the wealth of nations'. It recommends water as a safe investment. Annual revenues of the water industry are 40 per cent those of oil and more than pharmaceuticals. While at Enron, Rebecca Mark said she 'would not rest until all the world's water had been privatized'. The World Water Forum at The Hague in March 2000 was largely run by transnational corporations who had their eyes on big profits. *The New Internationalist* has highlighted the way in which Structural Adjustment Programmes (SAPs) imposed on poor countries by the IMF, have included water privatization as part of the package, benefiting the water companies. These companies want control of water resources and infrastructure, in some cases trying to close family wells and 'privatizing rain'!

Privatization

The key question is whether water is a need, which can be supplied on a for-profit basis, or whether it is a right which governments ought to supply to their citizens. The dogma is that public is inefficient and therefore bad; private is efficient and therefore good. While at the World Bank, James Wolfensohn was a typical spokesman, arguing that giving public services away to people leads inevitably to waste. A position paper for the Food and Agriculture Organization (FAO) recommends privatization on the grounds that water pricing sends the appropriate signals to ensure efficient use of water. In the view of its authors the fact that water is available free or at a price below its true cost of production is the cause of water scarcity. On the classic liberal account of economics as the management of scarce resources this seems to make sense. What it fails to address is the question whether wealth gives you rights, for example, to swimming pools and golf courses, and whether poverty means that you may have no rights, that is, you die. The World Development Movement (WDM) claims that 6,000 children die every day as a result of lack of access to clean drinking water.

It is clear, of course, that clean water is not free. It needs cleaning and filtering in order to make it safe and to prevent the spread of water-borne diseases. As the industrial revolution occurred and great cities developed, it was assumed that the cost of this should be met by a charge upon the rates, and cleaning be undertaken by public sector corporations. Today, in response to the great enclosure movement, it is argued again and again that only privatization can deliver clean water effectively. In fact there is no evidence that privatization has led to more effective water use. On the contrary, deterioration and depletion of the world's water systems have taken place concurrently with the rise in power of corporations and a global financial system in which communities have been disempowered. In Argentina when water was privatized water rates doubled. Water companies added to their profit margins but did not pass savings on to the consumer. When Chile privatized water, mining companies were given nearly all the water rights in that country free of charge. Today they control Chile's water market and the shortage of water has served to push up prices. Water privatization in Buenos Aires put the price of water up and led to the neglect of sewage treatment, because the provision of water was more profitable. When people in

Cochabamba, Bolivia, found they could no longer afford water, James Wolfensohn insisted that 'No subsidies should be given to ameliorate the increase in water tariffs'. All water users should bear the full cost of the water system. Mass resistance led the Bechtel subsidiary to back down and its subsidiary Aguas del Tunari left in 2000. Water provision has now been taken on by the community itself. However, Bechtel claimed 15 million dollars compensation for lost profits, which could destroy the local group now administering water services. The status of that claim is as yet unclear. Elsewhere Suez, Veolia and Thames Water are all using political and legal action to recoup losses and claim anticipated profits from contracts from which they have withdrawn. Under WTO rules the fact that water is a tradeable commodity means that quantitative restrictions on exports and imports are not allowed and that environmental concerns can be struck down as a 'disguised barrier to trade'. Governments have to prove they have adopted the approach least restrictive of the rights of foreign private water-providers, a clear example of putting corporate rights before those of ordinary people.

In 2005 a water privatization scheme in Africa which was meant to be a flagship for the whole process collapsed. The World Bank funded a scheme, supported by the British government, which was meant to supply Dar es Salaam with fresh water. The Tanzanian government claims that no new pipework has been installed and that water quality has decreased and they have therefore cancelled the contract. The company, City Water, is suing the Tanzanian government for breach of contract. Tanzania was forced to privatize its water as a condition of international debt cancellation. The World Development Movement claims that the IMF forced water privatization on people to benefit western water companies. The British government paid the free market organization Adam Smith

International, a quarter of a million pounds to produce a video which told people that 'privatization brings the rain'. Currently the British government is urging water privatization on another of Africa's poorest countries, Sierra Leone.

These examples make clear that maximizing profits is the prime goal of corporations, not ensuring sustainability or equal access to water. Water is treated as a resource like any other based on the market dynamics of increasing consumption and profit maximization.

In a private market the superior purchasing power of large cities such as Los Angeles and of corporations such as Intel could force the cost of water up far enough to make water so expensive that it is out of reach of small farmers, towns and indigenous peoples. The model of privatization creates enormous disparities of power between corporations and the local governments that usually deal with them. The World Bank urges water stamps for the poor as a way of helping those who cannot pay, but such charity is often non-existent and punitive. At the heart of the privatization viewpoint is the assumption that all resources must be captured and made available for sale in order to increase monetary wealth. But to do so we tamper with natural systems that have balanced the earth's ecosystems for millennia. Furthermore, for-profit corporations are less publicly accountable and transparent than elected governments. As CEOs have noted time without number, no matter how ethically inclined they might be, their main responsibility is to increase profit for their shareholders.

As noted in the second chapter, the Bretton Woods Institutions largely exist now to forward the work of corporations. Poorer nations find it hard to resist their pressure. The IMF required Rwanda to put the country's water and electricity company under private management by June 2001. In Honduras it required a 'framework law' for the privatization of water and sewage services and told Nicaragua it had to increase its water and sewage tariffs by one and a half per cent a month on a continuous basis. Furthermore, the results of water-testing, which were public knowledge when publicly owned, now become 'confidential intellectual property' belonging to 'the client', so that the amount of *E. coli* infection in water, for example, is not made known.

Water and shalom

In his poem 'Ozymandias', Percy Bysshe Shelley gives a withering account of the illusions of human power. A wrecked statue surrounded by desert bears the legend:

> 'My name is Ozymandias, king of kings:
> Look upon my works, ye Mighty, and despair!'
> Nothing beside remains. Round the decay
> Of that colossal wreck, boundless and bare
> The lone and level sands stretch far away.

Sandra Postel points out that many ancient civilizations disappeared because the agricultural heartlands which supported them withered up due to salinization. The arrogance of modern humanity overreaches that of ancient kings. Postel is obviously right that we need to double water productivity and get twice as much benefit from each litre if we are going to feed eight billion people. She gives many examples of both low and high-tech methods for increasing water efficiency such as micro-irrigation, which decreases the risk of salinization and produces better crop yields, and the use of treadle water pumps which allow small farmers to irrigate their land effectively. She estimates that with technologies known and available, agriculture could cut its demands by up to 50 per cent, industries by up to 90 per cent and cities by one third, with no sacrifice of economic output or quality of life. The efficiencies Sandra

Postel details are essential if we are going to survive but in themselves they are not the answer. At essence what is required is a culture change in our approach to our world.

Because water is the foundation of life – 'holy' as the Church has termed it – it cannot be administered on a purely for profit basis. Of course it is not 'free': its cleansing and transport incurs a charge, and water prices can send 'signals' about its real value, to use market jargon, but this should be democratically administered. Locally controlled and publicly owned water supply schemes in Bangladesh, Brazil and Ghana have shown that community water management can provide clean water at cheaper rates than private firms. In Argentina co-operatives have demonstrated they can be efficient providers in cities of fewer than 50,000 inhabitants and have good quality services and more affordable prices. Water is a public trust, to be guarded by all levels of government, and access to an adequate supply of clean water is a basic human right.

The Conference on Water for People and Nature held in Vancouver in 2001 recognized this in issuing the following declaration:

> We proclaim these truths to be universal and indivisible:
> That the intrinsic value of the Earth's fresh water precedes its utility and commercial value, and therefore must be respected and safeguarded by all political, commercial, and social institutions,
> That the Earth's fresh water belongs to the Earth and all species, and therefore must not be treated as a private commodity to be bought, sold, and traded for profit,
> That the global fresh water supply is a shared legacy, a public trust, and a fundamental human right, and therefore, a collective responsibility.

Water is part of the common treasury which cannot be alienated. It is too precious a resource to be processed and distributed according to profit principles. What the recognition of water scarcity calls for is more co-operative economic and political paradigms. Without these the chances of human survival are increasingly bleak. 'We have lost a sense of respect for the wild river,' writes Sandra Postel, 'for the complex workings of a wetland, for the intricate web of life that water supports. By and large, water has become strictly a resource to be dammed, diverted, and drained for human consumption.' In Christian terms what has been lost is the sense of gratitude which underlies our entire life. In 1937 Karl Barth wrote a book called *Justification and Justice*, setting out the Christian grounds for opposition to national socialism. He understood that the fundamentals of our faith embrace the whole of life, and do not just apply to Sundays. Grace, we may say, is a political principle. To understand that is to learn a very different way of administering and sharing water to that currently in place.

For further reflection and action

- What does it mean practically that water is 'holy'?
- Who profits from the water we use?
- Is there anything we can do for water-scarce regions?
- Is water a gift or a commodity?

5

Tilling and keeping

————◦•◦————

In a famous article written in 1967 Lynn White, Jr traced the deep roots of the environmental crisis to the Christian attitude to nature. 'What people do about their ecology', he noted, 'depends on what they think about themselves in relation to things around them. Human ecology is deeply conditioned by beliefs about our nature and destiny – that is, by religion'. He believed this to be as true in 1967, in the so-called 'post-Christian West' as it had been in the Middle Ages. White argued that it was the victory over pagan animism which allowed people to exploit nature in a mood of indifference to the feelings of natural objects. He suggested a return to the alternative view of St Francis who tried to 'substitute the idea of the equality of all creatures, including man, for the idea of man's limitless rule of creation'. He pointed the finger especially at the so-called 'dominion' text, Genesis 1.28, where God says to the first couple:

> Be fruitful and multiply, and fill the earth and subdue it; and have dominion over the fish of the sea and over the birds of the air and over every living thing that moves upon the earth.

White could find support for his argument in Brian Griffiths, Margaret Thatcher's policy advisor. For him, 'These verses suggest very clearly that God created the physical world for our use and pleasure, with sufficient resources for our needs and with a specific commission to harness the resources of the natural world for our benefit'. Quite to the contrary, I would suggest, when read in context and in the light of tradition. As we saw, Winstanley spoke of domination, but this meant one thing with a world population of perhaps 350 million, and very limited technology, on the one hand, and one of several billion and the resources of steam and electricity, not to mention nuclear energy and genetic modification, on the other. White (and Griffiths, in an ignorance only too typical of contemporary evangelical theology) overlooks the extent to which reformed theology was a theology of grace, and therefore opposed precisely to any exercise of domination. It also overlooks the basic rule of interpretation, that a text must be read in its context. In this case, the redactor who arranged the material in Genesis quite deliberately followed the first creation account with the second, which spoke of human beings as gardeners, not dominating, but placed in the garden to till and keep it. The second text effectively tells us how to read the first.

In complaining of an exploitative attitude to nature, however, White has a legitimate point. He correctly implies that ethics, too, are part of our ecology. Life is a whole and cynicism or indifference at one point is bound to be reflected elsewhere. Exploitation of the natural world usually goes together with exploitation of other humans. What the God of life calls us to is respect for life, as Albert Schweitzer called it. For him ethics was 'infinitely extended responsibility to everything that lives'. We saw in relation to food that according to the Genesis redactors creation as a whole was originally vegetarian and that the permission to kill came much later. This should not, of course, be understood to contradict evolutionary history. Rather it is an expression of an understanding of reverence for life which extends, as we have become increasingly aware, to the whole of creation. Precisely here is the worry with regard to farming for, corresponding to the kind of reading of Genesis 1 which worried Lynn White, although we have agricultural practices which are deeply exploitative, we also have more sustainable practices. These resemble the two ways that the Deuteronomists set before their people, a way of death and a way of life, practices of domination on the one hand and tilling and keeping on the other. Before looking at these in more detail we must first consider the situation of farming at the start of the third millennium.

Farming in the third millennium

Since the neolithic revolution most humans have been engaged in growing food, and this was true beyond the middle of the twentieth century. Only in the past 60 years has the balance tipped towards urbanization and industrialization. In that period the number of farms in England dropped from half a million to 158,000.

The rate of decline has not noticeably eased: over 17,000 farmers and farm workers – five per cent of the workforce – left the land in the 12 months to June 2003 and more than 80,000 jobs have been lost in the past decade. All sectors of farming and cultivation have been affected. There has also been a huge decline in the numbers of those who grow their own food. During the early twentieth century in Britain there were just under four million acres of allotments producing about half the fruit and vegetables consumed domestically. There are now under 40,000 acres.

The same story applies to Europe as a whole, where in 1999 200,000 farmers gave up agriculture. France lost half its farmers between 1982 and 1999. In Germany a quarter have gone in the past ten years. The US has lost four million farmers since the 1930s. On the other hand Asia has 385 million farms, Africa

36 million, Central America six million and South America ten million. Worldwide, two and a half billion people work in agriculture, so it is still the world's largest single source of work. About a third of the world's population is still supported by traditional and 'unimproved' agriculture.

One of the main reasons for the huge fall in numbers is that farmers worldwide have been unable to make a living, caught between rock-bottom prices for their products and rising costs for inputs. In the US between 1987 and 1997 farmers received 123 billion dollars for their animal and crop products, but paid 185 billion in production expenses. In Britain ten years ago a British pig farmer made nine pounds profit per pig. In 2002 he lost an average of three pounds per pig. Sheep farmers have for some years paid more to have their sheep sheared than they can get for the fleece. Fifty years ago in Britain the equivalent of 50 to 60 pence of every pound went back to farmers. Today nine pence in the pound goes back to them. Many products are sold for less than the price of the product, and milk costs less than bottled water. In 2005 British farmers are getting 15 pence a litre for milk. The crisis affects all sectors – cereal, dairy, poultry and livestock.

Globally the price index of commodities declined by 47 per cent between 1982 and 2001. In sugar alone exporters to the global market lost nearly two billion dollars due to falling prices in the four years up to 2002. Less than ten per cent of the retail value of coffee stays with the countries that grow it, whereas ten years ago they kept 30 per cent of its value. Auction prices for tea in India have fallen by a third in the past six years and the tea-workers union has had to negotiate a 12 per cent wage cut. Low rice prices have affected rural economies in Thailand, Vietnam and China. A World Bank study estimates that the divergence between the farm and retail prices costs commodity exporting countries more than 100 billion dollars a year and that anti-competitive behaviour by the dominant transnational corporations is the key cause. The situation is exactly as it is represented in the book of Proverbs: A poor man's field may produce abundant food, but injustice sweeps it away (Proverbs 13.23).

In Europe and North America there is a perception that farmers have been featherbedded by subsidies, but the truth is that subsidies have gone to the biggest farmers. Under the previous terms of the Common Agricultural Policy seven farms received payments of more than half a million pounds. Eighty per cent of UK farm subsidies went to 20 per cent of farmers with the largest farms. The smallest 30,000 farmers received a third of all support and poultry and pig farmers did not qualify anyway. Even under the new single farm payment size is still disproportionately rewarded. In the US only 120,000 farms, out of a total of two million, receive 60 per cent of all income. Subsidies have been very selective, therefore, and in any case, the cost of inputs has meant that by and large they have ended up in the pocket of agribusiness.

Practices of domination

With ever-increasing momentum over the past half-century, mechanization and 'efficiency' have favoured large farms. The average agricultural area keeps increasing as smaller scale farmers find they cannot make a living and sell up, with their bigger neighbours, or corporately owned farms, buying their land. These big farms are very efficient at producing food. UK farms, for example, produce three times the amount of wheat and barley per hectare and more than twice as much potato and sugar beet as they did in the 1940s, and cows produce twice the milk per lactation. In Europe just 12 per cent of all farms produce 60 per cent of all agricultural output and a mere one per cent rear 40 per cent of all animals. In Britain ten per cent of farms produce 80 per cent of the food. However, this efficiency is only part of the story. It has a cost and the question is whether it is truly efficient and whether the gains are worth it.

Specialization

A first problem is that this kind of farming is on the whole monocultural. Farmers specialize in one thing, whether it be cereals, livestock or poultry. Sometimes the specialization is even more narrow, so that one farmer will rear pullets and then sell them on to someone who keeps laying hens; or livestock is sold on to be fattened and killed and so forth. It involves what Brewster Kneen calls the 'trivialization' of agriculture, 'the transformation of agriculture into a manufacturer and supplier of component parts for the transnational food assembly corporations'. Monocropping is supposed to be more efficient because it allows for economies of scale. But monocultures fail to respect the checks and balances which characterize the natural world, as Rachel Carson noted in *Silent Spring*. The traditional mixed farm has more effective resistance to pests and diseases. The more thoroughgoing the monoculture the less resistance there is.

The mixed farm was efficient in that it was able to grow food for its animals and use their manure on the fields. Cattle feedlots, by contrast, have to find ways of getting rid of the manure they produce and import food for their animals. A cattle feedlot with 20,000 cows produces as much sewage as a town of 320,000 people. In Texas there are cattle feedlots with up to 100,000 animals! The fuel required to dispose of all this waste must be considerable.

Monocultures rely on high inputs both in terms of fertilizers, pesticides and cattle feed. In 1994 every acre of wheat in

Britain received an average of eight sprays. Of course these inputs help explain the rise in productivity, but against that the cost of removing agrochemicals from water is nearly 120 million pounds per year. US agriculture, hugely reliant on pesticides, is also highly efficient at producing food, but agricultural run-off into the Gulf of Mexico means that it can no longer support marine life. In Spain the downside of a highly 'successful' horticulture development is that nitrate levels are ten times higher than the World Health Organization advises. Thirty per cent of acid rain in the Netherlands is a product of the country's industrial livestock operations. The Royal Commission on Environmental Pollution, reporting in September 2005, called for further research into the impact of pesticides on human health and dismissed the idea that there are 'no scientific concerns' about spraying. Many illnesses and allergic conditions, and possibly cancer, may be linked to it. If you cannot buck biology, you cannot buck ecology: everything goes somewhere.

Keeping animals in huge numbers means they cannot be reared on their normal diets: cattle feed on grass, pigs root around and poultry peck around for grubs and grains. At present it takes seven kilograms of cereals to produce one kilogram of feedlot beef, four kilograms to produce one of pork and two kilograms to produce one of poultry. Currently, livestock consume as much grain as two billion people, meaning that we are already looking at the task of finding food sufficient for eight billion people, and this is set to increase exponentially. Thus, if meat consumption stays at its present levels it will not be eight billion people we have to feed by 2050, but 10 billion and more.

Industrialization

Industrialized agriculture, working on the assumption that 'farming is a business like any other' Taylorizes production.

Adam Smith famously eulogized the division of labour in a pin factory and this principle was one of the key factors in the industrial revolution. Many people, however, feel that this is deeply distasteful in farming since it implies an instrumentalization of living creatures. Battery farming is the most notorious example, where poultry are reared in sheds holding up to 50,000 birds. Each bird has an area the size of an A4 sheet of paper, and may never see daylight. Keeping livestock in overcrowded conditions also leads to stress and aggressive behaviour. As we saw in Chapter 4, keeping animals on this scale – getting them to grow faster than they would normally, to have more offspring than they would normally and to produce more milk – requires huge quantities of antibiotics. American farmers give six times more antibiotic than is used in human medicine to their livestock, purely as growth promoters.

Industrial farming has also led to the loss of biodiversity. In China there were 10,000 wheat varieties in 1949; in 1979 only 1,000 remained. In the US 95 per cent of cabbage, 91 per cent of field maize, 94 per cent of pea and 81 per cent of tomato varieties have been lost. Loss of biodiversity is not simply an aesthetic issue. It could also be life-threatening in that we become dependent on a small number of crops which could fall prey to disease. In the last 50 years in Britain, 60 per cent of ancient woodlands, 90 per cent of meadows and 50 per cent of birds that depend on agricultural fields have gone. One-third of 6,500 breeds of domesticated animals are under threat of extinction. Two-thirds of England's hedgerows were lost between the 1950s and the 1990s. In the developing world the Green Revolution likewise led to the loss of thousands of native varieties, which were substituted with monocultures of rice, wheat and maize. Not only did the number of crops cultivated shrink, but the range of cultivated varieties shrank as well.

Traditionally farming has been about good husbandry, following good practice in the care of animals and the rotation of crops. The well-publicized disasters of the past two decades are linked to what Colin Tudge calls 'cut price husbandry' and to making farming subservient to the market. BSE, for example, is caused by rogue proteins called prions which cause brain deterioration and are transmitted by ingestion. Cattle are of course herbivores, but they are given feed supplements to fatten them up, to make them grow more quickly, or to produce more milk. These supplements included produce from dead animals and it seems likely that this was the ultimate cause of BSE. When the disease turned up in human form as CJD, panic set in and British farmers lost £1.6 billion in cancelled exports. Farmers had been trapped by 'economics'. The reason for giving such feed was to maximize output and minimize costs. No instances of BSE have been found in organic herds. The practices which led to BSE are a classic example of disrespect for life which backfired very quickly on those who adopted them.

The foot and mouth epidemic in 2001, which was the worst in recorded history, and which was even more expensive than BSE, was not caused by poor husbandry, but was bound up with technocratic and bureaucratic approaches to agriculture. Millions of healthy animals were slaughtered in the policy of contiguous cull, driven by completely fatuous computer modelling of epidemics and even more by the fear that prices of exported meat would be cut. The slaughter policy, applied in a profoundly inhumane way, which involved in one case fetching a small flock of (healthy) sheep out of the house where the owner had tried to protect them was, again, a clear expression of disrespect of life. The trucking of animals, partly because of the closure of small local abattoirs, but also to cash in on EU payments, helped spread the disease around Britain. The final financial cost was eight billion pounds, but a much higher toll was taken in ruined lives, farmer suicides, wrecked communities, and the loss of many small businesses dependent on rural tourism.

Accidents

Industrial agriculture, true to its model, seeks to reduce labour to a minimum. In a matter of decades this has led to a situation where rural communities have disappeared. Farmers lead the suicide tables and the rates for the number of accidents at work, while soaring house prices driven by wealthy commuters make it impossible for agricultural workers to find anywhere to live. All over the world there is a race to the bottom in the conditions of agricultural employment. A Friends of the Earth report in June 2005 concludes that supermarkets' need to push prices down is forcing suppliers to use labour which is poorer, more desperate and likely to be more compliant. The report concludes that there is a direct connection between concentration of retail power and deterioration of working conditions. Investigation into the activities of gangmasters has shown that abusive, evasive and fraudulent activities are frequent, including non-compliance with minimum wage legislation, unlawful deduction from wages and use of illegal immigrant labour.

Industrial agriculture is also highly energy dependent. If total world agriculture production and food-processing were based on European and North American levels of energy use, known oil reserves would be exhausted in 30 years. Industrial agriculture contributes to carbon emissions directly through the use of machinery, and indirectly through the oil used to produce and transport fertilizers and pesticides.

For all these reasons the claims of industrialized agriculture to be truly efficient have to be challenged. Is there an effective alternative in a world of six or eight billion people?

Tilling and keeping

It is often suggested that we cannot survive without hi-tech agriculture, but advocates such as Jules Pretty, Professor of Environment and Society at the University of Essex, suggest that on every count smaller ecological farms may be more efficient than their large industrial neighbours and may produce better crop yields. Vandana Shiva also argues that 'small ecological farms have productivity hundreds of times higher than conventional farms'. This is the crucial question. We cannot afford to be romantic about agriculture. Although in Britain agriculture is explained as being essentially about park-keeping and farmers are encouraged to turn to alternative crops for bio-fuel and so forth, farming essentially is about food – about feeding the world's people. Precisely for that reason, though, the present trend towards ever larger units using ever fewer people needs reviewing. The question for the future must be what counts as true efficiency, and present rules of accountancy cannot give the answer to that. New measures of efficiency are required, and it may be, as Tudge, Pretty and others suggest, that good husbandry is the key to success rather than better technology.

Taking the problems involved in industrial agriculture one by one we can see how they match up when set alongside the small mixed farm. In the first place, mixed farming keeps checks and balances in place. There is less chance that disease will affect every aspect of a farm's production. Rotation of crops means that the lifecycle of pests is disrupted. Integrated pest management finds ways of dealing with pests which is not solely reliant on chemical sprays. Beekeepers, for example, have found that introducing mesh floors to their hives is a more effective way of dealing with varroa than the annual use of one or other of the patent chemical insecticides. Planting a wider range of crops is also a hedge against the more erratic weather that global warming is bringing.

Second, mixed farms recycle their wastes and make more effective use of their resources. They pay more attention to nitrogen fixation and soil regeneration. In other words, they rely more on good husbandry than on the agrochemical companies, an independence which may prove crucial as more and more of the food chain falls under corporate control. They also rely on far fewer inputs than industrialized agriculture. Where monocultures need 300 units per 100 units of food, polycultures need only five.

The small farm has no need to Taylorize production. As they have always done, farmers know their animals and their individuality. François Dufour, General Secretary of the Confédération Paysanne notes:

> If you drive your car at breakneck speed, with savage acceleration, it won't last so long. The same is true of intensively reared cattle. Farmers are encouraged to drive their herds to the maximum of their capabilities rather than to treat them prudently, with due regard to their health. Intensive milk production means that a cow, on average, has about three calves in a lifetime of a little over five years. With our form of sustainable farming, cows live for more than ten years.

Respecting animals is not sentimentality. If there is a moral ecology in which 'everything is connected to everything else' then we are sure to pay for disrespectful practices. To treat animals as items on a production line does damage to the whole of society, for ultimately we cannot live schizoid lives. The call for a more integrated agriculture, therefore, is also a call to live with greater integrity across the board.

Mixed farms not only make less impact on the environment; it has been calculated that organic agriculture produces between 75 and 125 pounds of positive externalities per hectare, in terms for example of the preservation of hedgerows, biodiversity and topsoil. 'Give me spots on apples but leave me the birds and the bees' sang Joni Mitchell, in response to Rachel Carson's polemic against the blanket use of DDT. In costing these things we have to bear in mind the huge financial significance of rural tourism, worth some 20 billion pounds per year in the UK, where there are a staggering 430 million day visits to the countryside each year, and 33 million overnight trips. Beauty may not be truth but it certainly generates wealth!

Again, small, mixed farms generate more robust rural communities and on the whole employ more people. Given that eight billion people cannot all live in cities and find things to do there, the question of human community, and what people are meaningfully going to do, is quite as urgent as the question of how people are to be fed. Jules Pretty has documented the growth of community food systems and rural partnerships around the world which both develop more vibrant local communities and are involved in massive increases in agricultural productivity using locally adapted and sustainable technologies. He speaks of the emergence of foodsheds: self-reliant, locally or regionally based food systems comprised of diversified farms using sustainable practices to supply fresher, more nutritious foodstuffs to small-scale processors and consumers to whom producers are linked by the bonds of community as well as economy. The growth of farmers' markets around Europe and in North America may be an instance of these arriving on our doorstep.

Finally, small-scale agriculture is nowhere near as energy dependent as industrial agriculture, a key factor in a world faced by global warming. Agriculture plays a significant part in global warming through deforestation, fertilizer use and the methane from cattle and rice paddies. Sustainable farming can do much to reduce these emissions. For all these reasons small, mixed farming may be more truly economic than anything achieved by economies of scale.

Joan Thirsk, in her *History of Alternative Agriculture*, shows that agriculture has gone through many cycles over the last 700 years, now going for big units, now for small. She thinks we are ripe for another round of small-scale, more labour-intensive agriculture. Many of the ideas tried now, like set-aside, have been tried before. She argues that the strong assumption of our age that omniscient governments will lead the way out of economic problems will not serve. She believes that solutions are more likely to come from below, and she quotes William James:

> I am against bigness and greatness in all their forms, and with the invisible, molecular, moral forces that work from individual to individual, stealing in through the crannies of the world like so many soft rootlets, or like the capillary oozings of water, and yet rending the hardest monuments of man's pride, if you give them time. So I am against all big organizations as such, national ones first and foremost; against all big successes and big results; and in favour of the eternal forces of truth, which always work in the individual and immediately unsuccessful way, underdogs always, till history comes, after they are long dead, and puts them on top.

After a century of industrial agriculture, Jules Pretty argues that the time has come for the next agricultural revolution, a return to tilling and keeping and an end to practices of domination.

For further reflection and action

- Does our Sunday school or the local primary school visit local farms?
- How much are local growers paid for their produce and how does this compare with what you pay for it?

- Is there a local Community Supported Agriculture Scheme you could join (ring the NFU office), a box scheme your church could facilitate or a farmers' market you could support?

- What do you think of the pros and cons of intensive farming on the one hand and of sustainable agriculture on the other?

- Invite a local farmer (preferably farming no more than 200 acres) in to talk to the congregation about the situation in farming.

6

Harvest of the sea

Until the beginning of the twentieth century there were no problems with fish stocks. Boats were small and fishing was often dangerous. Fishermen hunted for fish by following the gulls or the whales. By and large the technologies of early twentieth-century fishermen differed little from those used by the first disciples, a fact which was recognized in fishing lore. Norfolk fishermen used to cast their nets 'in the name of the Lord', recalling the story in John 21. Even well-informed thinkers in the nineteenth century, like Jean-Baptiste de Lamarck and Thomas Huxley, assumed that the resources of the sea were infinite and were not worried by Malthusian predictions. Their confidence seemed more than justified when a glut of herring in the second and third decades of the twentieth century drove many Atlantic fishermen out of business. Two factors have changed this situation. First, with the doubling of world population since 1950 demand has soared, standing currently at over 130 million tonnes and set to expand to 180 million tonnes. Demand has in turn been stoked by the ease of supply associated with new marine technologies which began to be introduced after World War II. The 'success' and 'efficiency' of these technologies has produced an ever-more severe crisis in fishing worldwide, which calls into question the feasibility of the market as a way of managing human resources. Put together, as a fine Canadian study has suggested, these two factors seem to call for an urgent application of the sabbath and jubilee laws to fishing.

The crisis in world fishing

The new technologies which were introduced after World War II included echo sounders, longlines which might be 100 miles long and hung with thousands of baited hooks; purse seine nets, which encircle a shoal and are then hauled up; and factory ships. The first such ship, the *Fairtry*, was British and was commissioned in 1954. She was 254 feet long and displaced 2,800 tons. Soviet ships which displaced 8,000 tons soon followed, with nets which could hold several jumbo jets, and which could catch 100 tons of fish per hour. The new technologies catch not only the fish intended but many other species as well, including dolphins. This unintended catch is known as 'by catch' and, since it is thrown back into the sea, as 'discard'. These technologies are so 'efficient' at catching fish that the target species, say cod or sardine, is quickly fished out and it is then necessary to fish down the 'trophic level'. *Trophe* is the Greek word for food, and the trophic level refers to the fact that fish feed on the next species down; fishing down the trophic level means that as one species is fished out fishermen turn to the next species down, on which the other species depended. The new technology can also fish a mile down and often damages the ocean bed and fish breeding grounds. Such practices eventually destroy the capacity of the marine ecosystem to support the fishery. Global warming is also an issue affecting the ecosystem. The Laboratory for Science of Climate and Environment in Paris suggests that if carbon dioxide is produced at current levels, the entire southern ocean will become so acidic that the shells of marine creatures will dissolve, which would impact on the whole food chain. Salmon, mackerel, herring, cod and baleen whales all rely on this source of food.

Signs of disaster

Signs of disaster have been around for more than 40 years. The California sardine fishery celebrated by Steinbeck in his 1945 novel *Cannery Row*, and which was worth £1.5 billion in 1936, had ceased to exist by 1962. By 1968 the catch of northern cod reached a maximum of 810,000 tonnes landed; catch rates began to decline as overfishing took its toll. Spawning stocks of North Sea cod have plummeted from a high of 277,000 tons in 1971 to 59,000 tons in 2001, a level which cannot sustain commercial fishing. The same story was true for salmon, whose sea feeding grounds were found in the 1950s. New types of gear again led to huge catches and by the mid 1970s, 2,700 tonnes of salmon were being taken annually and salmon numbers began to fall. Bluefins (tuna) have also been overfished and their North Atlantic breeding populations are estimated to have declined by about 90 per cent since 1980. Menhaden, which provide the major source of fish meal in the US, used principally by the poultry industry, are also being fished out by commercial fisheries. If the stocks crash it is not simply a resource which is lost, but the job they do of cleaning the estuaries will no longer be done. Japanese trawler fleets have fished out the Western Indian fishing grounds and European fishermen are set to do the same for Africa.

Over the past 30 years a number of Food and Agriculture Organization (FAO) conferences have drawn attention to this aspect of the 'tragedy of the commons'. In 2005, a study it prepared found that global stocks of most fish were stretched to their limits. Nearly a quarter of commercial species have already been overexploited, with a total 70 per cent of species now being fished close to, at, or beyond their capacity. The logic of the market has driven this decline. Increased 'efficiency' in returning bigger catches has driven prices down. That in turn means that bigger catches are needed to pay for new ships and gear, for wages, and to make a profit. The circle which is supposed to be virtuous for the consumer actually ends literally in a dead end. Fishing communities have been destroyed all over the world – in India, Britain, Newfoundland and in the US. Sooner or later, as fleets fish lower and lower down the trophic level, fish will become an expensive luxury for the rich, if they are available at all. Currently the FAO estimates that fishery products account for 15 per cent of global animal protein intake, but this source could be destroyed by overfishing.

In response to this the FAO and the World Summit on Sustainable Development, held in Johannesburg in 2002, urged an ecosystem management approach towards fisheries, going beyond simply limiting catches. This involves the attempt to understand the whole marine context, including human beings as part of that. Managing world fisheries would then seek to hold all factors in balance in such a way that a worthwhile harvest could still be taken while not threatening fish stocks. Some have argued that this is too little, too late. In their view the situation is so serious that sustainability is the wrong goal because it involves sustaining seriously depleted fish populations. What they want instead is an application of the jubilee principle, which would allow 'rest' to marine populations for some years until they were restored to healthy levels. Just such a principle was applied successfully to North Sea herring in the 1980s and currently this population is not in crisis.

Who stewards the sea?

With the agricultural commons we saw that in the traditional system commoners zealously policed their ground. This has always been much more of a problem for the seas. In recent times national navies have either accompanied trawlers, or attempted to warn off boats from limits which countries have applied, but it is almost impossible to do this successfully. Given that fish are no respectors of boundaries, and that they sometimes change their breeding grounds, there is an obvious role for an international organization like the FAO, but the UN has no means of enforcing its policies and relies on the good-will of its members. Precisely here Garret Hardin's tragedy arises. Fishing plays a major part in many national economies, and in the world market as currently constituted, every nation is turned competitively against every other. Every nation feels duty bound to do what it can to protect its own fishing community and the upshot is that there is little or no incentive to conserve.

The multinational corporations involved in fishing are like-wise tied into competition. Because profit, not conservation, is their bottom-line and because they do not even necessarily have national homes, they are even more predatory than nations. They can exploit to the limit and then move on. Such corporations dominate the industry in many parts of the world, including Japan, Canada, the US and Britain. Canadian fishing companies have seen their profits rise as fish stocks have crashed, and have moved off to other seas – Russia, Alaska and Scandinavia. The Scottish branch of Friends of the Earth characterizes the corporations responsible for salmon farming there as driven by short-term economic priorities rather than long-term interest in the future of Scotland's environment. They argue that the search for profits makes the corporations indifferent to the problems raised by moving down the food chain. They have no obligation to stewardship. Fishing is 'an industry like any other' and like any other is supposed to be 'lean, mean and flexible', without large amounts of labour. This conventional business goal is inconsistent with maintaining the marine ecosystem.

Given the pressures on both nations and corporations others have argued, therefore, that the natural stewards of the sea are the traditional fishing communities all around the world, which use relatively low-tech methods, sell more or less locally, or which fish for subsistence. For these communities fishing has been a way of life for hundreds of years if not for millennia. These communities are place-based, governed by local knowledge and sustain fish stocks at a healthy level. Conservation is in their interest because both their livelihood and their culture is involved. Contrary to the market principle that the person with the biggest catch is the best fisher, a Newfoundland fisherman argues that the person who leaves most fish in the water should be considered the best fisher.

As with farming, the market seems the worst placed system to encourage anyone to act as steward. Markets cannot deliver the ecological justice which the FAO calls for because their concern is profit and the 'efficiency' (i.e. huge catches for least expenditure) which drives that. Ecological justice involves in the first place a recognition that the seas have their own integrity. Fishing, like the killing of animals, is a permission, something to be done with respect and gratitude. Such an attitude is also inconsistent with the destruction of the sea-bed and of coral reefs which is currently going on. Also, it requires us to think in terms of the common treasury. The sea and its stocks belong to all people and to the generations yet to come. To fish to extinction is an ultimately disrespectful practice.

Aquaculture

Given these facts, the need to try and farm fish is obvious, and aquaculture is now the fastest growing form of food production. In 2002 the farmed fish harvest was more than 51 million tonnes, with China accounting for an astonishing 71 per cent of that. According to FAO statistics, the contribution of aquaculture to global supplies of fish is now nearly 30 per cent. Aquaculture is growing more rapidly than all other animal food-producing sectors, most of the growth being in developing countries.

The development has not been without problems however. As with pigs and poultry, the need for profit means that fish are packed into their pens, and this promotes disease. In 1984 a new virus, carried by ships with live fish in their tanks, was detected in salmon farms in Norway; this virus then devastated Canadian and the North American fisheries. These viruses spread from farmed to wild salmon through escapees. Up to 40 per cent of North Atlantic salmon and 90 per cent in the Baltic are thought to be of farmed origin and the transmission of lice and disease from fish farms to natural stocks threatens the very survival of natural salmon. It is not only disease which is a problem. Genetically engineered fish grow bigger than their wild counterparts and are more effective at spreading their DNA. Unfortunately the offspring of modified fish are less likely to survive into adulthood, the so-called Trojan-gene effect.

Farmed salmon are also fed meals and oils from wild fish. Each pound of salmon requires at least three pounds of wild caught fish. There is, therefore, a net loss of protein in the marine ecosystem when wild catch is converted into meal. Fish farming also involves the use of some fodder diverted from crop production. Thus aquaculture competes with other human activity for productive land.

More serious still is the problem of pollution. The Friends of the Earth (FOE) report mentioned above found that salmon farming used toxic chemicals illegally, discharged contaminated untreated wastes directly into the sea and spread parasites and diseases around the coast. According to a 1999 calculation, for each ton of salmon produced, approximately 100 kilograms of nitrogenous compounds, including ammonia, was released into the sea. The estimated waste discharged from 340 Scottish fish farms in 2000 was equivalent to almost twice the annual sewage discharge by Scotland's entire human population. The result of the use of toxic chemicals is that farmed salmon have been found to have dangerously high levels of pollutants. A study in the Journal *Science* in 2004 found PCBs, dioxin, toxaphene and deldrin concentrations in farmed salmon, especially from Scotland. The report suggested that eating farmed salmon could result in exposure to 'a variety of persistent bio-accumulative contaminants' and warned that people ought not to go above one half-meal of salmon per month – and this in fish marketed for its health benefits! FOE Scotland concluded that when the losses in the angling and tourist industries, and in wild fisheries and shell fisheries, were taken into account, intensive sea cage fish farming may make neither economic nor ecological sense.

Finally, valuable wetland habitats have to be converted, which are nurseries of marine life. Aquaculture is a logical way to go in some ways but can in no way be regarded as the complete answer to global fish demand.

Implementing the Jubilee

With what seems from our perspective to be extraordinary pre-science, Israel extended its sabbath legislation to animals, and its Jubilee legislation to the land. In the same way it needs to be

113

extended to the sea. The seas and marine communities also need a sabbath rest to ensure their continued health and their role in the whole ecology of the planet. Jubilee laws of redemption are a way of resetting the balance to what it ought to be in terms of a healthy and sustainable marine community. Given the imprecise nature of fisheries science, and especially of stock assessment, the precautionary principle has been invoked. The Canadian study already mentioned, however, also argues for an 'adjacency principle' alongside the precautionary principle on the grounds that it is traditional fishing communities which have the best idea of what is going on. The study argues, first, that ecosystems function from the bottom up and damage to them can also first be observed at local level; that local people have detailed harvesters' knowledge of their own fishery and its attendant ecology; and that unlike large fishing corporations with their mobile fleets and even more mobile capital, coastal communities are not 'footloose'. The authors agree that bottom-line economic thinking is not a good ethical foundation for policy. On the contrary, managing fisheries sustainably is part of the fundamental human right to food security. They also point out that urban areas are overcrowded and cannot employ everyone. To destroy fishing communities for short-term gain simply exacerbates already grievous problems in human ecology. Fishing communities, like agricultural communities, need both to survive and even to grow, rather than to be decimated or eliminated, as is currently happening.

The present state of the world's fisheries is perhaps the most compelling evidence that the principles enunciated by Adam Smith so modestly, but now applied so immodestly, simply do not work. Economics is part of a whole moral ecology and to flout that, and to let the market take the place of ethical decision-making, is to court disaster. What is called for in its place is considered, democratic, economic decision-making, based on a respect for the needs of all people and on the needs of the live creatures on which we depend. Only such principles can guarantee the human future.

For further reflection and action

- How do you think the harvest of the sea should be managed?
- Does the Jubilee legislation still have relevance in the modern world? If so, how can we make it relevant?

7

Playing God

—•◦•—

Although many notable scientists have been clergy or religious, including Mendel, the founder of genetics, it is also true that the Christian Church has a poor record in terms of obscurantist opposition to scientific advance. We only have to think of Galileo, of the encounter between Bishop Wilberforce and Thomas Huxley, and today of the influence of creationists in American education. Both on account of this history and on account of the fundamental principles of their own faith, it ill behoves Christians to oppose science – a fact recognized by the Jesuits who were Galileo's contemporaries, who firmly supported his research. Not for nothing do Christians believe that the Logos – word, or reason – became flesh. Science is only possible at all because the universe is a rational place. Theologically speaking it is the Logos, the Word of God, which expresses itself in the order of the universe.

This is not to say, of course, that Christians should embrace any science whatsoever. The more powerful the science the more urgent the ethical questions, as the question of nuclear power above all has taught us. Genetic engineering is another such issue on which, as with nuclear power, opinion is sharply divided. Consider these two opposed views on GM technology, the first from a Deputy Secretary of the United States Department of Agriculture. For him,

Biotechnology is our greatest hope . . . It dramatically increases crop yields. It uses less water and pesticides, offers greater nutritional value. And, in this process, there's less stress on fragile lands and forests . . . Food biotechnology is already making its presence felt. It's filling consumer demand with high quality, good tasting food products produced in ways that are environmentally sustainable.

This view is shared by Tony Blair and many other modernizers, who believe that GM crops offer us a brave new world.

On the other side Brewster Kneen, the Canadian farmer and campaigner on food issues, writes:

Genetic engineering is an expression of ingratitude and disrespect, if not contempt. It is a vehicle, in practice, of an attitude of domination and ownership, as expressed in the assumption that it is possible, reasonable, and morally acceptable to claim ownership over life. The claim that it is possible to own life, at least to the extent of being able to claim a patent on a life process or life form, is so outrageous socially and ethically as to be hardly worth debating.

Well, the claim that GM issues are hardly worth debating is clearly premature given the extent of the current debate! At issue between the two sides are questions about the nature and the role of science, but above all the question of power. The industrial revolution which has given us the immense advantages of the modern world has to a large extent relied on scientific discovery. It is impossible to deny the benefits which this has delivered. On the other hand, the very success of natural science has bred an attitude which has allowed for the exploitation and domination of the natural world in complete disregard of the social and ecological consequences. It has bred the idea that if something can be done it should be but, as the Faust story illustrates, science without ethics represents a pact with the devil. Science betrays itself when it becomes a practice of domination.

The debate about GM

Genetically modified crops are plants which have an alien gene inserted into the genome to give them a certain trait. The technique is not precise. The new gene is fired into the host and so the result is quite literally 'hit or miss'. The technology involves crossing species barriers never before crossed so it is not, as is often claimed, simply an extension of traditional cross-breeding. The germ plasm of the crop, once genetically engineered, becomes permanently altered.

GM technology as developed so far has been put to a number of uses: it is used to allow plants to resist herbicides, so that farmers can spray weeds, but leave the crop unaffected; to either kill or deter pests; to increase drought-tolerance; to provide additional nutrients such as vitamin A in rice; and to produce pharmaceuticals. Advantages include the possibility that crops will need less spraying, and that wastage of crops, currently running at 40 per cent, could be reduced to five per cent. Again, given increased water scarcity, drought-resistance could be exceptionally valuable. One can see why advocates are so starry eyed about it. Unfortunately, there are also serious problems. The first and most serious of these is that, in the words of Arpad Pusztai, the plant researcher sacked from the Rowett Institute, and Malcolm Hooper, formerly Professor of Medicinal Chemistry at the University of Sunderland, 'the science has not been done'.

Arpad Pusztai's case is one of the most glaring scientific scandals of recent times. He was a leading researcher employed by the Rowett Institute in Aberdeen, widely regarded as a nutritional scientist at the top of his field. Working on methods for approving GM foods he found, first, that GM varieties were very unstable, and that plants in the same group, from the same parent, might have significantly different protein levels. Second, he found that rats fed with GM foods suffered damage to their immune systems. He also found that the 'research' done by biotech companies like Monsanto was shoddy and would not pass rigorous scientific scrutiny. His results unfortunately co-incided with an EU meeting which sought to endorse the use of GM. Under huge political pressure, possibly involving 10 Downing Street, Pusztai was sacked, gagged, vilified by the Royal Society, and had his house and office burgled. The medical journal *The Lancet* came to his defence, despite threatening phone calls from a member of the Royal Society who, it turned out, had extensive links to the biotech industry. Its view was that 'Governments should never have allowed these products into the food chain without insisting on rigorous testing for effects on health. The companies should have paid greater attention to the possible risks to health'.

What *The Lancet* acknowledges is precisely what Pusztai and Hooper argue; that there is a lot going on with gene expression which is not understood. Due to the shifting nutritional make up of GM foods, as illustrated by Pusztai's research, accurate and reliable safety assessments of any kind may be impossible. Genes may trigger allergies and promote cancer formation or viruses, and bacteria may recombine to produce new pathogens. Novel toxins may produce both direct and indirect effects. For example, in March 1999 York Laboratory scientists discovered that soya allergies skyrocketed. The soya used at that time was mostly imported from the US and was genetically modified. Starlink maize, which was not supposed to be eaten by humans, but which had been labelled safe for commercial reasons, caused severe reactions. Claims by biotech companies that their products are safe have to be handled with maximum caution. Monsanto had said both Agent Orange and PCBs were safe, but they were not. They are linked to cancer, neurological disorders and birth defects. Pusztai himself was an advocate of GM crops, but as a scientist he was committed to rigorous testing. He and other concerned scientists would argue that, given our current lack of understanding of the consequences of GM technology, GM food is not a safe option.

Another problem is that unlike conventional insecticides that are used at specific moments, transgenic plants produce toxins continuously, thereby exposing insects to them on a constant basis. Common sense suggests that this cannot but help promote further insect resistance. Even more dangerous, antibiotic-resistant genes may transfer resistance to antibiotics to humans. New viruses could be created which are resistant to all penicillins. The World Health Organization has documented the emergence of resistant salmonella, campylobacter, and *E. coli* types. The use of herbicides and pesticides which involve organophosphates and nerve agents like sarin can affect gene activation, hormone response and energy production. Use of herbicide-tolerant crops virtually guarantees that beef, poultry and pork will have higher contamination levels of selected pesticides than such livestock had previously. With the bio-concentration factor that operates for many of these herbicides, people will be exposed to a largely untested and different burden of pesticides than before. Malcolm Hooper concludes, 'It is difficult to conceive of a more potentially damaging target for compounds destructive to human health and well being' than those related to current GM modification.

Again, agricultural biotechnology threatens to decrease the number of crop plant varieties currently grown by substituting a few varieties for the many now in use. It is likely to lead to monocropping and the loss of plant genetic diversity. As argued in Chapter 5, this may well increase the fragility of the crop and permit the introduction of widespread disease. Vandana Shiva argues that should terminator technology ever be widely introduced, it may very well spread to surrounding crops and could introduce global sterility. Given nature's incredible adaptability, she argues, this threat must be taken seriously. For all these reasons some argue that the risks are so severe the precautionary principle is not adequate. Such technologies, it is argued, should not be used at all unless there is an overwhelming necessity. As it is, with the huge increase of genetically modified food in the US and elsewhere, some believe that we are backing ourselves into an evolutionary corner.

Choice?

Quite apart from the problem of risk, there is the extraordinary contradiction that in a world dedicated to 'choice', it is impossible to stop contamination of non-GM crops. GM plots are only separated from non-GM plots by 400 metres, but bees fly three miles. Maize landraces 60 miles away from GM crops have been contaminated. An organic company in the US is suing the US Environmental Protection Agency because there has been cross-pollination with GM. In July 2005, modified genes from crops in a GM crop trial in Britain transferred into charlock, creating a 'superweed' which is pesticide-resistant. Transference of GM crops has been a problem in Canada, where farmers have been unable to get rid of unwanted rape. To stop their farms being overwhelmed with superweeds Canadian farmers have had to resort to older and stronger herbicides, now outlawed. Some, like Naomi Klein, have argued that the real agenda is to achieve so much genetic pollution that there will be no GM-free food. The burgeoning use of transgenic food crops, she argues, constitutes a non-consensual experiment on a mass scale, which affects the transformation of basic staples and may have a huge impact on ecosystems and human well-being. Given the use of soya in sweets, chocolate bars, ice cream, biscuits and salad dressing, this seems only too plausible. Choice is also denied by the refusal of the Food and Drug Administration in the US to allow labelling of GM foods. As early as 1992 they decided, again without the science being done, that there was no substantial difference between GM and non-GM food. Testing has been abandoned since then, left instead to voluntary 'consultations' between companies and the FDA.

George Monbiot points out that Monsanto will never repeat the mistake of seeking to persuade consumers to purchase its products. The company has spent ten billion dollars buying up seed producers and companies, including Seminis, the biggest producer of vegetable seeds in the world. In 1999 Monsanto estimated that in five years 95 per cent of seeds would be genetically modified. In some places, farmers must purchase GM seeds or plant nothing at all. The issue is control of the food supply, a standard imperialist tactic throughout history. At some point they will simply be in a position to ensure that GM foods are sold and consumed wherever they say they will.

Does it work?

Ironically, for all the hype, GM technology by no means always works. Bollworm infestation in GM cotton in the US, for example, was up to 50 times the level that usually leads to spraying. Thirty thousand acres of cotton were lost and cotton farmers subsequently sued Monsanto. Similarly, conventional soya is still outperforming the GM varieties. GM crops are also much more expensive. Argentina, one of the biggest producers of GM soya has found that it is trapped in dependency. 'The more we produce the poorer we become,' said one of its leading agronomists. GM yields, now covering 90 per cent of all Argentine production, are ten to 15 per cent less than conventional varieties. In India, Cargill's hybrid sorghum cost Rs 3,230 per acre and delivered a return of Rs 3,600 per acre. Indigenous seed cost Rs 300 per acre and the return was Rs 3,200 per acre. The claim that GM is needed to feed the world is therefore likely to be false simply on the grounds of its real efficiency. Behind many of the claims the desire for profit is fairly transparent. For example, the production of yellow rice to deal with vitamin A blindness is not a real need. It turns out that one carrot covers the whole daily requirement, as does between 100 and 200 grams of spinach, dandelion, kale, or coriander leaf, especially if augmented with a few drops of red palm oil. Colin Tudge points out that such blindness does not occur in traditional societies. It is in fact caused by western economics – the shift away from self-reliant agriculture to cash crops. In his judgement yellow rice is 'expensive, much hyped but at bottom fatuous'. In the same way better irrigation could utilize land much more efficiently without the need to use GM crops.

Science, patents and power

Given all these problems, why is GM being promoted so vigorously? The answer is money, power and profit. Jeffrey Smith has documented the extraordinary political pressure brought to bear on those who oppose GM food. I have already mentioned what happened to Arpad Pusztai (and his wife, who was also involved in the research). Monsanto threatened the printer of *The Ecologist* magazine with legal action for an issue dealing with their products and the journal had to find another printer. Journalists have been dismissed and hounded through the courts for revealing flaws in GM. In Canada notes and files critical of scientific data provided by Monsanto were stolen from a locked filing cabinet in a researcher's office. The *Times Higher Education Supplement* in September 2000 reported that 30 per cent of scientists working in either government or recently privatized research institutes in the UK had been asked to change their research conclusions by their sponsor. The US Committee on Science considers anyone who opposes GM a 'political activist'. The four leaders of the biotech industry – Monsanto, Dow DuPont and Novartis (now Syngenta) – gave more than $3.5 million in political donations, three-quarters of it to Republicans. Twelve congressmen who had stalled a bill requiring labelling of GM foods had collectively taken $711,000 from companies with dairy interests, four directly from Monsanto. Hardly surprising, then, that Henry Miller, in charge of biotech issues at the FDA from 1979 to 1994, said 'the US government agencies have done exactly what big agribusiness has asked them to do and told them to do'.

Science trades on the idea of objectivity, of pure 'disinterested' science. In this respect Pusztai was an old-fashioned scientist. In truth there has always been less disinterested science than we might like to believe, but corporate power is skewing the direction of scientific research as drastically as formerly communist and fascist governments tried to do. The accusation of 'playing God' does not refer so much to forms of science which try to recreate life from its fundamentals, but more to a new version of absolutism. The question to put to science today is whether it exists for the common good, for example, to see that there is food security for eight billion people, or whether it exists to help make huge profits for a small number of corporations and their shareholders.

This issue is in many ways focused around patents, or as they are more commonly known now, 'intellectual property rights'. Patents seek to reward inventiveness and one can see the point.

When someone makes a fortune from a stolen idea we consider it unjust. Most people are happy with the caricature idea of the slightly mad inventor, the 'Professor Branestawm' character who patents some ingenious but not hugely significant idea. The patenting of life-forms, however, which began in the US in the 1980s, has a completely different moral significance.

All patents (even Professor Branestawm's) stand in tension with an older idea that knowledge exists for the human good and should be shared freely. Einstein acknowledged that he 'stood on the shoulders of giants'. This was an acknowledgement of the fact that knowledge never begins *de novo* but is a social and historical product, presupposing the labours of countless generations. Patents deny this social dimension. They rest on the illusion that an inventor (these days usually a corporation) is 'an island alone unto itself'. An earlier Indian Patent Act recognized this in refusing to patent socially useful products. This act has been replaced by a new act mirroring US patent laws, forced on the country by globalization. Indira Gandhi expressed the older view in arguing that patents should not apply to medical discoveries and that people should not profiteer from life and death. That her view is widely shared is evidenced by the indignation felt when immensely rich drug companies sought to prevent the use of cheap anti-viral drugs in Africa. That seemed to be an abuse of the patent system.

This abuse is linked to the rise in corporate power. It was under corporate pressure, especially from biotech corporations, that the WTO agreement on Trade Related Intellectual Property Rights (TRIPS) was framed in 1995. They effectively wrote the agreement. A huge increase in the number of patents has been generated since then, many concerned with food and farming. Today, 97 per cent of all patents are held by companies in western countries. A report on the US patent office in 2001 spoke of new patent applications falling off shelves, piled into corners and crowding every desk. Patents, it said, were the new American gold rush. The relationship between the patent office and the biotech firms was said to be 'incestuous'.

In effect, firms involved in biotechnology promote a new form of enclosure no longer of common land but of knowledge. Such an enclosure, like the other forms we have already reviewed, expresses an instrumentalist approach to life itself, but more fundamentally there seems to be a moral blindness attached to trying to make a profit out of the means of life, as Indira Gandhi implied. The standard defence, of course, is that profits are ploughed back into research, which cannot happen without them. But corporate profits, CEO incomes and shareholder returns tell a different story. Vandana Shiva cites evidence to show that only 15 to 20 per cent of research costs are recouped through patents. The growth of intellectual property rights also rests on the Smithian idea that people will only ever do something if they can make a profit from it. Profit, in this narrative, is the driver of human progress. Such an idea could only be propagated by people with no knowledge of the history of science, and it is a cynical and despicable account of what it means to be human.

Many of the claims to patent are profoundly specious and involve what Shiva calls 'biopiracy'. Biotech companies use plant varieties that are the product of years of cross-breeding by farmers, or which represent millennia of accumulated knowledge. The brass face of these companies knows no bounds. They have sought to patent basmati rice and neem, known and used in India for centuries. Monsanto has claimed patent rights on soy plants in China. Their latest bright idea is to patent the pig! Monsanto is seeking patents not only on methods of breeding but on actual breeding herds of pigs as well as the offspring of that result in more than 160 countries. They are describing very general methods of cross-breeding and selection, using artificial insemination and other breeding methods which are already in use. Effectively these companies tinker a little with traditional processes, the common heritage of humankind, and then apply for a legal patent. Companies like Monsanto have proved themselves exceptionally aggressive in pursuing their legal 'rights'. The Saskatchewan farmer Percy Schmeiser, for example, was successfully sued by Monsanto because rape seed which blew into his field grew there and was considered Monsanto's property.

Shiva, again, speaks of this process as a new form of colonialism, seeking like its older and cruder form, to create dependency. As patent law works out it actually prevents the transfer of technology from north to south. Shiva argues that patents should be compared to the medieval bull granting Latin America to the Spanish crown: 'The duty to incorporate savages into Christianity has been replaced by the duty to incorporate local and national economies into the global marketplace, and to incorporate non-Western systems of knowledge into the reductionism of commercialized Western science and technology'. The new colonialism works through seeds, extracted from developing countries in the first place and then sold back to those who can afford them. The creation of dependency through food has been an avowed aim of US foreign policy for a long time. In 1957 vice-president Hubert Humphrey told a US audience, 'If you are looking for a way to get people to lean on you and to be dependent on you in terms of their co-operation with you, it seems to me that food dependence would be terrific'. In 1974 the US Department of Agriculture Secretary told the World Food Conference in Rome that food was 'one of the principal tools in our negotiating kit' and an important weapon (!). What has happened in the interim is that power has shifted to the corporations, yet the strategy remains the same.

Above all the question is one of the exercise of inappropriate power. Four biotech companies own 44 per cent of patents on the world's most important food crops. Syngenta, DuPont and Monsanto account for nearly two-thirds of the global pesticide market, almost one-quarter of the global seed market and 100 per cent of the transgenic seed market. As we have already seen at a number of points, the food chain is falling under the control of an ever-smaller number of corporations. Brewster Kneen, Canadian farmer and food campaigner, writes:

> If five or six corporations have control over every seed of all major commercial crops planted anywhere on earth, this is totalitarian. Add to seeds control over the genetics of all major lines of commercial animals and it will be somewhat more totalitarian. Then engineer all the genetics – plant or animal – to be hybrids, sterile or both, and the achievement will be without question totalitarian. It will amount to the occupation of the land – the earth itself – by foreign troops and their local mercenaries.

By claiming global monopoly patent rights throughout the entire food chain Monsanto seeks to make farmers, food producers, and ultimately consumers, entirely dependent and reliant on one single corporate entity for a basic human need. The issue, as former Environment Minister Michael Meacher has recognized, is power. What is at stake is the question of who controls the means of life and production.

The hallmark of the good society, according to the Jewish and Christian scriptures, is shalom, justice and peace. When the prophets attacked their own societies what they criticized, over and over again, was the arrogation of power by the rich, appropriating to themselves the means of life, which in their day was primarily land. Today, in addition to land, it is knowledge. The prophets were driven by a vision in which God had gifted the land to everyone. In one strand of Israelite thinking Israel's election did not mean they would end up as 'top nation', but rather that the Jew was the typical human being. 'Every person under their vine and fig tree' was therefore a vision of every human family with sufficient to live by and in control of the means of production. It is that vision which underlies the critique of both the way GM technology has been developed and the corporate drive to make profits by patenting knowledge. The world in which corporations rule, which is as much a command economy as ever Stalin's was, needs to be replaced by decentralized democratic economies in which farmers and rural communities have much more of a say. The director of Novartis agreed that GM technology would not feed the world, and that what was needed for that was political will. The Green Revolution likewise failed because the problem is primarily not one of agricultural technology but of maldistribution. Only real empowerment among those who are currently hungry will enable us to enjoy the peace which scripture holds up as the human goal.

For further reflection and action

- How is the grace of God known in our scientific practice?
- Is it morally right to own patents on seeds?
- Should we be pressing ahead with GM crops?
- How can democratic control of the food chain be re-established?

Conclusion

How should we celebrate harvest in the age of the global market? The first thing to say is that, of course, harvest is a service of thanksgiving as it has always been, a service of celebration with joyful hymns and music. To live by grace is to live by gratitude, and nowhere more so than here. Harvest is the opportunity to relate the eucharist to the whole food and farming economy. It is also the opportunity to recall Jesus' wider practice of table fellowship with a harvest supper which celebrates local food prepared to the best of our ability, opened up free of charge to those we know to be marginal in our area. Harvest is the last occasion when we should have 'school dinners' as they have been known to generations of unfortunate schoolchildren. As I have insisted earlier, good food does not have to be expensive food. Poor congregations are not condemned by fate to eat unhealthy food or unappetizing food. If we understood the implications of our incarnational faith properly, perhaps cookery clubs might be understood as a part of mission!

At the same time any harvest celebration has plenty of room for penitence. Many if not most congregations in the West will belong to that 20 per cent of the champagne-glass society who have more than 80 per cent of the world's wealth. We are trapped into supporting exploitative and unsafe labour practices by our shopping patterns, if not by our share ownership. Most of us in the West are part of the consumer society which uses so much of the earth's resources and which Alan Durning speaks of as the most fundamental change in the day-to-day existence of the human species in the whole of its history. As all

130

of our prayers of confession recognize, repentance calls for change of practice. If we are serious about celebrating harvest, we have to learn to shop differently and to challenge the social responsibility codes of our leading supermarkets. From day one Christianity was about lifestyle. That challenge comes to us especially at harvest as we celebrate the material world. The goal, as Durning puts it rather beautifully, 'is not ascetic self-denial, but a sort of unadorned grace'.

Prayer leads to action. Simply to commend the poor of the world into God's hands and go on living as we have always done is not an option. The action which prayer at harvest leads to is manifold. In the first place we have to support our own beleaguered farmers. Churches can become drop-off points for local box schemes. Where possible they can join CSA (Community Supported Agriculture) schemes. Sunday schools, especially in urban churches, can contact local farms and help educate children about the whole farming process either by inviting a farmer in to talk or, if possible, through a farm visit. More widely, churches can sign up to show solidarity with the Small and Family Farms Association in Britain, or with the Via Campesina internationally, and keep themselves abreast of campaigns. Speaking about a church-based food scheme in Canada, farmer Dan Wiens wrote:

> When you go into Safeway and buy cabbage for ten cents a pound you don't see the farmer, and if you can get it for eight cents, you buy it. In our case, when the people know you and they see our cabbage for ten cents a pound, and they have experienced what it is like to weed cabbage, they say, forget it, I'm not going to pay you ten cents, I'm going to pay you twenty cents. That is exactly what has happened. We are adding culture to agriculture. We're putting some humanity back into it.

In this case, church action on food played a part in the regeneration of community. If that is not celebrating harvest effectively, I don't know what is.

Throughout the book we have seen that issues around climate change are crucial to harvest. The 'ecocongregation' scheme has been running for some years now, but a disappointingly small number of congregations are signed up to it. How can we say we are concerned about God's earth if we do not operate our own churches by a rigorous environmental audit? It is not difficult to do. It is an important sacramental step. Churches and congregations should think about their ecological footprint: this can be reduced by changing our shopping, travel and heating patterns. Beyond that churches need to stand in solidarity with the environmental NGOs like Friends of the Earth or Greenpeace. Parishes might consider a community subscription and include their work in their community education.

As we have seen throughout this book, both climate change and farming are bound up in the closest possible way with the dominant modes of economic expression. The forms of trade to which our own governments are committed, which they use our taxes to further, are profoundly unjust. Try measuring them by the standards of the prophetic books which we read in our liturgies. The argument that these books were addressed to peasant societies without modern means of production is deeply unconvincing in view of the spread of wealth which these policies bring about. When we vote for our governments we are effectively voting both for the continuance of massive injustice and for the continued plundering of the planet. Few Christians are really happy with that outcome.

Something can be done by supporting groups which campaign on trade, like the World Development Movement. Christian Aid, Cafod and Oxfam, which many churches already support, have produced incisive critical reports over the past 30 years. They have moved from primarily acting as distributors of aid, to raising our consciousness about such issues. Congregations have some way to go, however, before they catch up with this move. More deeply, congregations need to reflect on their vocation to be a contrast society. If God's good earth is not going to be destroyed by human greed then a huge change of political culture is needed, for the political forms we have, rooted in the eighteenth and nineteenth centuries, no longer do the job.

Christian communities helped towards the last change in political culture with the emergence of workers' parties, at the end of the nineteenth century, and if they are alive to the Spirit, then they should help towards the change we so urgently need now. Groups opposing globalization have come together under the slogan, 'Another World Is Possible'. Could one find a better one-line summary of Paul's letter to the Romans? That Christians do not see this is due to a centuries-long tendency to privatize religion and understand it purely in terms of piety. But Paul's vision of an alternative world had huge effects, as the eighteenth-century historian Gibbon recognized. Perhaps we no longer quite believe in the world-changing dimension of incarnation and resurrection.

Oscar Wilde remarked that the trouble with socialism was that it took too many evenings. Awareness of the magnitude of the problems we face, and the need to campaign on such a wide front, can make life dour and joyless – graceless, in fact. Precisely here comes the point that we live by faith. God asks us to do what we can, not what we cannot. There is no doubt that the situation is urgent, even critical, and that idleness and complacency is not a possible Christian response. At the same time, when we commit ourselves to pray and act then we are free to rejoice in God, to celebrate the God of life, with our neighbours, in song and dance, food and wine. That is God's vision for us, and it is the proper rubric for harvest.

Bibliographical notes

Chapter 1

Winstanley's writings can be found conveniently excerpted in *G. Winstanley: Selected Writings* (1989). Patristic arguments about property are set out in Charles Avila's study *Ownership* (1983). Ulrich Duchrow and Franz Hinkelammert have a compelling analysis both of property and of Locke's contribution to the argument in *Property* (2004). Garret Hardin's famous argument is to be found in *Science* 162: 1243–8 (1968). For climate change I have drawn on the Carbon Trade Watch paper *Hoodwinked in the Hothouse* by various authors, and on Heidi Bachram's paper *Climate Fraud and Carbon Colonialism* as well as on the annual *State of the World* reports published by the Worldwatch Institute. Mark Lynas' *High Tide* (2004) offers a journalistic account of the effects of climate change around the world, and Dinyar Godrej's *No Nonsense Guide to Climate Change* (2001) sets out the facts and arguments clearly. Throughout I have made use of Colin Tudge's marvellous *So Shall We Reap* (2003), for which this book is not intended as a competitor. It really is required reading. Alan Thein Durning's *How Much Is Enough?* (1992) remains a very important attempt to relate the ecological crisis to the consumer society.

Chapter 2

For information on the role of corporations the best book among a burgeoning literature remains David Korten's *When Corporations Rule the World* (1995) and its follow-up, *The Post Corporate World* (2000). On corporate involvement in agriculture I have used Action Aid 'Power Hungry: Six reasons to regulate global food corporations' (2005), and Bill Vorley's, *Food, Inc.* prepared for the

UK Food Group. On finance capital I have used Michael Rowbotham's illuminating *The Grip of Death* (1998). On trade, two of the most useful books are John Madeley *Hungry for Trade* (2000) and Graham Dunkley *Free Trade* (2004), which points out that there are at least four major economic paradigms still under discussion. On economic alternatives a compelling vision is offered by James Robertson, *The Sane Alternative* (1983) and *Future Wealth* (1989). Herman Daly's *Steady-state Economics* is the best introduction to his theories, while H. Daly and John Cobb, *For the Common Good* (1990) is the best single volume on green economics and theology. On growth Richard Douthwaite's *The Growth Illusion* (1992) remains the best single book alongside the older *The Costs of Economic Growth*, by E. J. Mishan (revised 1993). Jawara and Kwa, *Behind the Scenes at the WTO* (2004) is one of the many books which gives an idea of how the WTO actually operates. Ulrich Duchrow's *Alternatives to Global Capitalism* (1995) spells out the Christian critique of capitalism. On supermarkets, Friends of the Earth prepared an important briefing, 'The Tesco Takeover' in June 2005.

Chapter 3

On food I have used Felicity Lawrence's *Not on the Label* (2004) as well as her many articles for *The Guardian*. Eric Schlosser's *Fast Food Nation* (2001) is standard reading. Greg Critser's *Fat Land* (2003) also has material on fast food. Tansey and Worsley, *The Food System* (1995), does what it says on the tin, as it were. I have also used Peter Brown's wonderful *Body and Society* (1988). José Bové and François Dufour give an account of the French struggle for local food and more sustainable farming in *The World Is not for Sale* (2001).

Chapter 4

On water Sandra Postel's work is fundamental, especially in *The Last Oasis* (1992) and *Pillar of Sand* (1999) as well as in her contributions to State of the World Reports. In addition readers could look at Barlow and Clarke, *Blue Gold* (2002). I have also consulted a report prepared for the FAO by J. T. Winpenny, 'Managing Water for Water Security' (1996) which tells us, among other things, that the chance of anyone dying of starvation in the future is 'remote to vanishing'.

Chapter 5

On agriculture Colin Tudge's work is presupposed throughout, as well as Jules Pretty, *The Living Land* (1998) and *Agri-Culture* (2002) Herman and Kuper's *Food for Thought* puts the point of view of the Confédération Paysanne. Brewster Kneen's *The Rape of Canola* (1992) *From Land to Mouth* (1993) and *Invisible Giant* (1995) spell out the role of corporations in farming as does Jansen and Vellema's *Agribusiness and Society* (2004). Jerry Buckland, *Ploughing up the Farm* (2004) charts the impact of neo-liberalism on agriculture. *Bringing the Food Economy Home* suggests alternatives. John Madeley's *Food for All* (2002) also looks at the need for a new agriculture. Christopher Booker and Richard North's *Not the Foot and Mouth Report*, published by Private Eye, documents this murky, and now almost forgotten episode. I have also consulted the report chaired by Sir Don Curry, *Farming and Food: A sustainable future* (2002). Joan Thirsk's *Alternative Agriculture* (1997) gives one some hope by putting the insanity of so much agricultural policy in historical perspective.

Chapter 6

Far and away the best book on the state of the world's fisheries is Harold Coward's *Just Fish* (2000). I have also used Richard Ellis' *The Empty Ocean* (2003), Stephen Sloan's *Ocean Bankruptcy* (2003), Mike Smylie's charming and informative *Herrings* (2004), and Friends of the Earth (Scotland)'s report *The One that Got Away: Marine salmon farming in Scotland* (2001). The varying usage of tons/tonnes in this chapter reflects the original sources' usage of either imperial or metric measures.

Chapter 7

For biotechnology I have used an unpublished lecture by Professor Malcolm Hooper, given in Exeter in 2004. In addition I have used Vandana Shiva, *Biopiracy* (1998) and *Protect or Plunder* (2001); Jeffrey Smith, *Seeds of Deception* (2004); Marc Lappé and Britt Bailey, *Against the Grain* (1999); Paul and Steinbrecher, *Hungry Corporations* (2003); Brewster Kneen, *Farmageddon* (1999) and de la Perriere and Seuret, *Brave New Seeds* (2000).

Bibliography

Action Aid, 'Power Hungry: Six reasons to regulate global food corporations', 2005.

Avila, Charles, *Ownership: Early Christian teaching*, London: Sheed and Ward, 1983.

Bachram, Heidi, 'Climate Fraud and Carbon Colonialism: The new trade in greenhouse gases' in *Capitalism Nature Socialism*, vol. 15, no. 4 (December 2004), pp. 1–16.

Barlow, Maude and Clarke, Tony *Blue Gold*, London: Earthscan, 2002.

Booker, Christopher and North, Richard *Not the Foot and Mouth Report*, London: Pressdram, 2001.

Bové, José and Dufour, François, *The World Is not for Sale*, London: Verso, 2001.

Brown, Peter, *The Body and Society*, London: Faber and Faber, 1998.

Buckland, Jerry, *Ploughing up the Farm: Neoliberalism, modern technology and the state of the world's farmers*, London: Zed, 2004.

Coward, Harold, Ommer, Rosemary, Pitcher, Tony, *Just Fish: Ethics and Canadian marine fisheries*, Newfoundland: Institute of Social and Economic Research, 2000.

Critser, Greg, *Fat Land*, Harmondsworth: Penguin, 2003.

Curry, Don, *Farming and Food: A sustainable future*, London: HMSO, 2002.

Daly, Herman, *Steady State Economics*, London: Earthscan, 1992.

Daly, Herman and Cobb, John, *For the Common Good*, London: Green Print, 1990.

Douthwaite, Richard, *The Growth Illusion*, Totnes: Green Books, 1992.

Bibliography

Duchrow, Ulrich, *Alternatives to Global Capitalism*, Utrecht: International Books, 1995.

Duchrow, Ulrich and Hinkelammert, Franz, *Property*, London: Zed, 2004.

Dunkley, Graham, *Free Trade: Myth, reality and alternatives*, London: Zed, 2004.

Durning, Alan Thein, *How Much Is Enough?*, London: Earthscan, 1992.

Ellis, Richard, *The Empty Ocean*, Washington: First Island, 2003.

Friends of the Earth, 'The Tesco Takeover', June 2005.

Friends of the Earth (Scotland), 'The One that Got Away: Marine salmon farming in Scotland, 2001.

Hardin, Garret, 'The tragedy of the commons', *Science*, 162: 1243–8, 1968.

Hopton, A. (ed.), *G. Winstanley: Selected writings*, London: Aporia, 1989.

Godrej, Dinyar, *The No-Nonsense Guide to Climate Change*, London: Verso, 2001.

Jansen, Kees and Vellema, Sietze, *Agribusiness and Society*, London: Zed, 2004.

Jawara, Fatoumata and Kwa, Aileen, *Behind the Scenes at the WTO* (rev. ed.), London: Zed, 2004.

Kneen, Brewster, *The Rape of Canola*, Toronto: NC Press, 1992.

Kneen, Brewster, *From Land to Mouth*, Toronto: NC Press, 1993.

Kneen, Brewster, *Invisible Giant: Cargill and its international strategies*, London: Pluto, 1995.

Kneen, Brewster, *Farmageddon*, Gabriola Island: New Society, 1999.

Korten, David, *When Corporations Rule the World*, Kumarian: Connecticut, 1995.

Korten, David, *The Post-Corporate World*, Kumarian: Connecticut, 1999.

Lappé, Marc and Bailey, Britt, *Against the Grain: The genetic transformation of global agriculture*, London: Earthscan, 1999.

Lawrence, Felicity, *Not on the Label*, Harmondsworth: Penguin, 2004.

Bibliography

Lynas, Mark, *High Tide*, London: Harper Perennial, 2004.

Madeley, John, *Hungry for Trade*, London: Zed, 2000.

Madeley, John, *Food for All*, London: Zed, 2002.

Mishan, E. J., *The Costs of Economic Growth* (rev. ed.), London: Weidenfeld and Nicholson, 1993.

Norberg-Hodge, Helena, Merrifield, Tod, Gorelick, Steven, *Bringing the Food Economy Home*, London: Zed, 2002.

Paul, Helena and Steinbrecher, Ricarda, *Hungry Corporations*, London: Zed, 2003.

De la Perriere, Robert and Seuret, Franck, *Brave New Seeds*, London: Zed, 2000.

Postel, Sandra, *The Last Oasis*, London: Earthscan, 1992.

Postel, Sandra, *Pillar of Sand*, New York: Norton, 1999.

Pretty, Jules, *The Living Land*, London: Earthscan, 1998.

Pretty, Jules, *Agri-Culture*, London: Earthscan, 2002.

Robertson, James, *The Sane Alternative*, Minnesota: River Basin, 1980.

Robertson, James, *Future Wealth*, London: Cassell, 1989.

Rowbotham, Michael, *The Grip of Death: A study of modern money, debt slavery and destructive economics*, Charlbury: Jon Carpenter, 1998.

Shepherd, Andrew, 'The Implications of Supermarket Development for Horticultural Farmers and Traditional Marketing Systems in Asia', Rome: FAO, 2004.

Shiva, Vandana, *Biopiracy*, Totnes: Green Books, 1998.

Shiva, Vandana, *Protect or Plunder*, London: Zed, 2001.

Sloan, Stephen, *Ocean Bankruptcy*, Guilford: Lyons, 2003.

Smith, Jeffrey, *Seeds of Deception*, Totnes: Green Books, 2004.

Smylie, Mike, *Herring: A history of the silver darlings*, Stroud: Tempus, 2004.

Tansey, Geoff and Worsley, Tony, *The Food System: A guide*, London: Earthscan, 1995.

Thirsk, Joan, *Alternative Agriculture a History*, Oxford: OUP, 1997.

Tudge, Colin, *So Shall We Reap*, Harmondsworth: Penguin, 2003.

Schlosser, Eric, *Fast Food Nation*, Harmondsworth: Penguin, 2002.

Bibliography

Smith, K., Ma'int, A., Keik, S., Gilbertson, T., Erion, G., Bachram, H., *Hoodwinked in the Hothouse*, Transnational Institute Briefing, no. 2005/3.

Vorley, Bill, *Food, Inc.: Corporate concentration from farm to consumer*, UK Food Group, London, 2004.

White, Lynn, 'The Historical Roots of Our Ecological Crisis', *Science*, 155: 1203–7, March 1967.

Winpenny, J. T., 'Managing Water Scarcity for Water Security', FAO, 1996.

Index

-----•◆•-----

Useful websites

Ecocongregation
www.ecocongregation.org
World Development Movement
www.wdm.org.uk
Via Campesina (a network of peasant farmers)
www.viacampesina.org
Friends of the Earth
www.foe.co.uk

142

Index